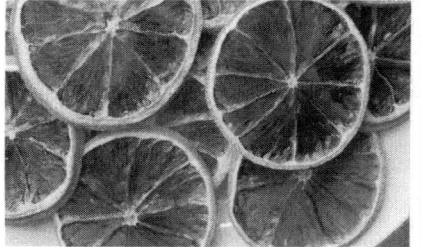

DEHYDRATOR
Cookbook For Preppers

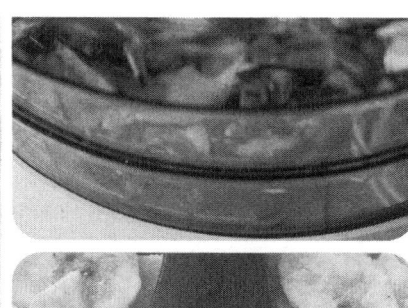

The Ultimate Low-Tech Guide To Preserve Fruit, Vegetable, Meat & Fish | How To Make Jerky, Fruit Leather, And Delicious Recipes For Just-Add-Water Meals

MELINDA BAKER

DEHYDRATOR COOKBOOK FOR PREPPERS

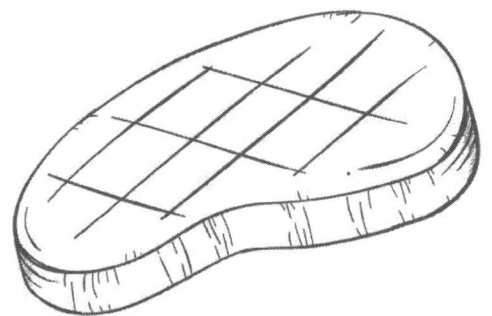

The Ultimate Low-Tech Guide To Preserve Fruit, Vegetable, Meat & Fish | How To Make Jerky, Fruit Leather, And Delicious Recipes For Just-Add-Water Meals

MELINDA BAKER

Copyright © 2022 by Melinda Baker
All rights reserved.

It is forbidden to duplicate, store, distribute, or transmit any portion of this electronic publication in any way—electronic, mechanical, digital, photocopying, recording, or any other—without the previous written consent of the publisher. Purchasers have agreed to use this electronic publication solely in line with the terms of use under which they purchased or transmitted it. This privilege is non-transferable, non-exclusive, and non-commercial in nature. In order to protect the rights of authors and publishers, it is a crime to participate in or support the pirate of copyrighted materials.

TABLE OF CONTENTS

INTRODUCTION

CHAPTER 1: FOOD DEHYDRATING FOR BEGINNERS

    Benefits of Dehydrating Food

    The Prepared Pantry

    One Year of Food Storage for a Family of Four

CHAPTER 2: DEHYDRATING METHODS

    Harness the Sun

    In the Oven

    Using a Dehydrator

    Microwave Drying

CHAPTER 3: BASIC DEHYDRATING TIPS

    Supplies Needed

    Dehydrating in Small Batches

    Dehydrating in Large Batches

    Blanching Vegetables for Dehydrating

    Fruit Pretreatments to Prevent Oxidization

    Food Touching on Trays

    Conditioning the Finished Product

    General Rehydrating Techniques

    Record Keeping

CHAPTER 4: FOOD SAFETY AND HYGIENE

    Select the Best Produce

    Clean Fruit and Vegetables

    What Not to Dehydrate

    The Effects of Light, Oxygen, Heat, and Humidity on Dried Food

    Using Frozen Vegetables

    Using Frozen Fruit

    Buying Large Quantities of Produce

<u>**CHAPTER 5: STORING YOUR DEHYDRATED FOOD**</u>

- Necessary Equipment
- Short-Term Vs. Long-Term Pantry
- Keeping Inventory
- Rotating Your Food

CHAPTER 6: FRUIT AND VEGETABLE LEATHERS
- Dehydrator Trays Liners for Making Leather
- General Instructions for Uncooked Fruit Leather
- General Instructions for Cooked Fruit Leather
- How to Store Fruit Leather
- What Can Go Wrong
- Vegetable Leather
- Highly Concentrated Food

CHAPTER 7: HOW TO MAKE JERKY
- Safe Jerky
- Prepare the Meat
- Pretreating the Meat
- Dehydrating the Jerky
- Creating Specialty Jerky Brines
- Storing Jerky
- Rehydrating Jerky in Meals

CHAPTER 8: SOUPS, POWDERS, AND HERBS
- Soups
- Powders
- Herbs

CHAPTER 9: DEHYDRATING 50 COMMON FRUIT AND VEGETABLES
- Apples
- Apricots
- Asparagus
- Bananas
- Beans (Green, Yellow, Snap)
- Beets
- Blueberries
- Broccoli
- Cabbage and Brussels Sprouts

- Carrots
- Cauliflower
- Celery
- Cherries
- Citrus
- Coconut
- Corn
- Cucumbers
- Eggplant
- Figs
- Garlic
- Ginger
- Grapes
- Green Onions and Leeks
- Horseradish
- Kale
- Kiwi
- Lettuce
- Mangoes or Papayas
- Melons
- Mushrooms
- Onions (Yellow, White, Red, Sweet)
- Peaches or Nectarines
- Pears
- Peas and Chickpeas
- Peanut (Raw)
- Peppers (Hot, Sweet)
- Pineapple
- Plums
- Potatoes
- Raspberries and Blackberries
- Rhubarb
- Spinach
- Strawberries

    Summer Squash

    Sweet Potatoes and Yams

    Tomatoes

    Winter Squash (Pumpkin, Acorn, Butternut, Delicata)

CHAPTER 10: DELICIOUS DEHYDRATOR RECIPES

    Blueberry Basil Syrup

    Pectin with Citrus Pith

    Pink Grapefruit Jelly

    Ginger and Lemon Infused Honey

    Honey Peach BBQ Sauce

    Slow Cooker Spiced Pear Butter

    Homemade Roasted Peanut Butter

    Creamy Cucumber Salad Dressing

    Tomato Powder

    Sweet Potato Powder

    Celery Salt

    Green Powder Blend

    Shredded Coconut

    Coconut Flour

    Strawberry Banana Rolls

    Cinnamon Apple Leather

    Pumpkin Pie Leather

    Pizza Blend Tomato Leather

    Mixed Vegetable Leather

    Tomato Wraps

    Sweet Potato Chips

    Kale Chips

    Zucchini Chips

    Dehydrated Refrigerator Pickles

    Beef Steak Jerky

    Cauliflower Soup

    Asparagus Soup

    Thermos Vegetable Soup

    Sweet Potato Coconut Flour Pancakes

Slow Cooker Stuffed Cabbage Rolls

Sautéed Winter Squash with Apples

Dehydrated Winter Squash Nests

Garlic Creole Spiced Squash Nests

Fajita Beans and Rice

Riced Cauliflower Pizza Crust

Hash Brown Mix in a Jar

Quick Brown Rice

Quick Cook Beans

Mrs. B's Stovetop Baked Beans

Mexican Fiesta Bake

Rose Hip Mint Tea

Orange Mint Tea Blend

Lemon Verbena Sun Tea

Lemonade with Dehydrated Citrus

Apple Crisp with Oat Topping

Steve's Low-Fat Pineapple Cake

Candied Ginger

Oatmeal Fig Cookies

ABOUT THE AUTHOR

MELINDA BAKER

INTRODUCTION

We do not know the name of the first master dehydrator, who recognized that apples left outside in intense sunlight could be preserved for later consumption. Their history is ancient, possibly as old as Egyptian culture, and lost to time. However, it is safe to say that drying food as a method of preservation has existed for as long as records have been kept. During the Middle Ages, Europeans constructed rooms as an extension of distilleries that were intended to dehydrate food using the heat of an indoor fire. Food was hung from the ceiling, smoked, and dehydrated. People living in a cool, wet climate were unable to dry food outdoors due to a lack of sunlight and dry days, but these specialized structures solved the problem.

By the middle of the 1800s, a method had been developed that allowed vegetables to be dried at 105°F and compressed into cakes. These dried vegetables were a welcome source of nourishment for sailors who endured lengthy voyages without access to fresh food. During World War II, dehydrated food was used as lightweight rations by soldiers serving on the front lines. Today, we refer to these as "meals ready to eat" (MREs). After the war, housewives did not rush to incorporate this compact, but frequently flavorless, food into their daily cooking routines, and dehydrated food fell out of favor.

The modern resurgence of dehydrated foods can probably be attributed to the backpacking community. Their demand for simple, lightweight, and nutrient-rich meals has generated a demand for prepackaged fruit, vegetables, side dishes, and full-course meals, as well as a renewed interest in dehydrating machines and other methods of drying foods. These new convenience foods are available at grocery and outdoor stores and are renowned for their simple preparation and short cooking time. The flavor has improved to the point where you would consider it a gourmet meal. Modern preppers have taken this challenge one step further by learning to produce, store, and rotate an entire year's worth of food.

This guide teaches the fundamentals of dehydrating fruit, vegetables, and protein; provides detailed information about drying 50 types of fruits and vegetables; and provides some tried-and-true, family-favorite everyday recipes. Included is everything you need to know to stock your own healthy, shelf-stable pantry.

As a gardener and prepper, I want to expand my pantry preparations beyond beans, rice, wheat, and egg powder. Dehydrating my garden harvest fills the void left by food that cannot be canned and a power-dependent freezer. Only a source of clean water and a fire stand between my family and a hot meal made with dehydrated ingredients.

This book is not only for seasoned gardeners, diligent food prepper, and expert preservers. It is for anyone who enjoys fresh food and wishes to participate in its preservation. To accommodate today's active lifestyles, dehydration must be simple to incorporate into your daily routine, take as little time as possible, and require minimal preparation. By purchasing in bulk, preserving in batches, and using an efficient dehydrator, you can dry food for daily consumption.

CHAPTER 1: FOOD DEHYDRATING FOR BEGINNERS

My husband and I decided to purchase a side of beef from a local farmer many years ago, when I was just getting serious about putting together a food storage plan. Our additional chest freezer was located in a detached garage about 20 feet from the house, and we filled it with all of the delicious cuts we had requested the butcher to wrap. This chest freezer contained enough frozen meat, vegetables, and fruit for months and months of home-cooked meals. It was fantastic and ridiculous.

When I went to retrieve a roast one day, I discovered that the kids had rummaged through the freezer several days prior and left the lid open. Yes, all of the food had thawed, and all of our hard work and money had been wasted, gone, ruined.

That day, I learned a valuable lesson about food storage. The rule of three in food preservation is to store food in at least three different ways, so as not to put all of your eggs in one basket. Having food in the freezer is essential, but learning how to process food in canning jars using a water bath and pressure canner is also essential. Dehydration fills the void and provides an additional method for properly storing food with a long shelf life.

Since that day, no food storage catastrophe has ever struck with such force. Canning, freezing, and dehydration are used to complete the process. If the jars break or the freezer is once again left open, we will not lose all of our food.

Benefits of Dehydrating Food

One of the reasons I enjoy dehydrating so much is that it is simple and requires a minimal learning curve to get started. You can successfully add dehydrated food to your pantry if you can chop food, blanch vegetables, and know what specific foods should look like when completely dehydrated.

When attempting to stockpile a year's worth of food, freezer space can be in short supply. Why waste that valuable space when you can dehydrate food without sacrificing quality? Dehydration frees up freezer space for more essential food storage items.

Dehydrated food has a much longer shelf life than canned food. When stored without oxygen, this food will be edible for at least five years. After one or two years, home-canned food may lose its color and texture, whereas dehydrated food maintains its quality. The shelf life of dehydrated food purchased commercially is sometimes as long as twenty years.

Moreover, unlike canning, dehydration requires minimal processing time. While my food is dehydrating, I am free to do other things, whereas I am practically tethered to the stove while canning. It takes the same amount of time to chop, but no additional time is required to watch the pot boil. Once the food has been cut and placed on the dehydrator trays, you can leave and check on the process several hours later.

Food that has been dehydrated is portable and weighs less than all other types of stored food. 70 to 95 percent of the food's water is removed during processing. It is the optimal choice for 72-hour kits and hiking or backpacking excursions.

Moreover, dehydrated food tastes great, and the drying process actually enhances the flavor. Frequently, food that has been reconstituted with water, juice, or broth appears and tastes as if it were freshly prepared. Using dehydrated food, you can easily make your own instant meal packages. Combine the ingredients into portions for two to four people and place them in Mylar bags with oxygen absorbers. It is simple to reach into the pantry and prepare a quick meal in minutes.

Bulk purchases of food items are less expensive, so if you buy in bulk and dehydrate your own food, you will save money in the long run on your grocery budget. In the United States, food prices increased by 1.1% in July 2017 and are projected to increase by 1.9% by 2020. Purchasing in bulk and dehydrating provide an advantage against food inflation. 1 Have a bag of spinach or lettuce that will expire before it can be consumed? Simply place it on a dehydrator tray to preserve it for later consumption. You will discover dozens of ways to save money by preserving food that would otherwise be wasted.

The Prepared Pantry

Do you plan what you will do with your garden's produce in advance? How many jars of tomato sauce will you need for the next three months' worth of meals? What about a year?

To have a well-stocked pantry, you must plan your pantry and create an extensive food supply. For some, that will be a three-month food supply, while others will require a one-year supply. This extended supply of food, acquired at the best price or grown yourself, will protect you from economic hardship just as effectively as your savings account will. It is best to preserve these items during their peak season and at their lowest price. Comparable to setting the lowest price for food to combat inflation. If I can save even 20 cents per pound on an item we regularly consume, it is worthwhile. What is twenty cents in savings for an item you use frequently, such as yogurt? It costs a family of four $208 per year to consume a cup of yogurt every weekday. That is $208 that could be used to pay off debt or purchase additional food.

Start stocking your stocked pantry with the items you use most frequently. This could be pancake mix for some families, applesauce or cream of mushroom soup for others. My family's food supply always includes spicy mustard, a variety of sauces, and salad dressings. Then we could do without, but why would we? Planning ahead makes it possible.

For this to be cost-effective, you should only store foods that you regularly consume. It is not a wise investment if the item sits on your shelf and spoils. The can of jellied cranberries that has been sitting in your pantry for the past year has reached the end of its shelf life and will be discarded, resulting in a loss of money. What use could you make of it? Fruit leather could have its shelf life increased by adding applesauce and spices.

For the most well-stocked pantry, stock both frozen and shelf-stable foods. Utilize this book to learn the fundamentals of dehydrating and how to freeze fruits and vegetables. Master water bath and pressure canning techniques. As previously stated, food should always be stored in at least three distinct ways. Then, if a natural disaster knocks out your power for a week, you may lose the contents of your freezer, but you will have canned and dehydrated foods in your pantry. Thus, you will still be able to eat, and the financial loss will be mitigated.

Ultimately, making a daily trip to the grocery store defeats the purpose of a well-stocked pantry, which is to always have access to healthy food and to save money. Refer to the Pantry Essentials chart below for a list of pantry items that will serve as a foundation for your ultimate stocked pantry.

In addition to the essentials, you should stock a variety of canned, dehydrated, and frozen fruits and vegetables that your family will enjoy and that can be used to prepare quick meals.

Do you carry an assortment of spices? I believe that the size of our spice cabinet is the key to the success of our pantry. If you have a variety of herbs and spices that you can combine in various ways, you can create a multitude of individualized dishes. Ground beef can be served multiple times per week if you have a variety of seasonings to create unique dishes. Once or twice a year, we purchase our spices in bulk from The San Francisco Herb Company (https://sfherb.com). They have spice mixtures and individual herbs and spices that I am unable to cultivate at home.

One Year of Food Storage for a Family of Four

My pantry is stocked and rotated in accordance with the "store what you eat" tenet, so we preserve and store foods that we enjoy. This also facilitates meal preparation, as we can always access the ingredients for a home-cooked meal from the pantry. Dehydration is not our only method of food preservation, but it is the one we rely on most for foods with a long shelf life. We offer well-balanced and nourishing meals at all times. Our basic formula can be used to create a food storage plan for your family.

Begin by keeping a food journal for two weeks. Not only the meals, but also the ingredients used to prepare each dish. The majority of families rotate through a set of approximately 14 basic recipes on a regular basis. Maintaining a two-week meal rotation will reduce food fatigue (are we having this again?) and make it easier to rotate your food.

Here is an illustration. Take your preferred spaghetti dish, categorize the ingredients, and enter the recipe into a spreadsheet or on an index card. Note each ingredient in the recipe.

- 1 teaspoon garlic
- ½ cup cheese, shredded
- 1 (8-ounce) box biscuit mix
- 16 ounces fresh fruit
- 1 (16-ounce) box spaghetti
- 1 (15-ounce) can tomato sauce (or 15 ounces homemade sauce)
- 1 pound ground meat or premade frozen meatballs
- 1 tablespoon Italian seasoning
- 16 ounces fresh vegetables

Now, purchase enough of each of these shelf-stable ingredients to stock your pantry for a year's worth of this meal (assuming you will consume it twice per month):

- 24 teaspoons garlic
- 12 cups cheese, shredded

- 24 (8-ounce) boxes biscuit mix
- 24 servings dehydrated fruits × the number of people in your family
- 24 (16-ounce) boxes spaghetti
- 24 (15-ounce) cans tomato sauce (or dehydrated tomato powder equivalent)
- 24 pounds frozen or canned ground beef (or 2 #10 cans freeze-dried beef)
- 24 tablespoons Italian seasoning
- 24 servings dehydrated vegetables × the number of people in your family

Does stocking a single meal seem daunting? After identifying the 14 meals your family consumes on a weekly basis, you should gradually purchase individual ingredients during your weekly grocery shopping trips. Start with one month (two times each recipe), two months, or three months depending on your grocery budget.

Do this for each of the identified meals over the course of the two-week period. Each breakfast, lunch, dinner, and snack must be recorded. This method allows you to keep track of what you already consume, helps you break it down by ingredient, and allows you to determine the exact number of months your pantry should last. In addition, it is useful to know how many pounds of fresh fruits and vegetables must be dehydrated annually in order to supply the meals you consume. It is highly customizable, allowing you to tailor it to your precise needs.

You may find that breakfast and lunch require less frequent rotation than dinners. Several times per week, the majority of us are content with eating yogurt, cereal, eggs, or toast with jam. Start with five to seven of these recipes, but rotate dinners more frequently.

Using the food storage calculator at ProvidentLiving.com, you can obtain basic recommendations for the amounts of protein, carbohydrates, fruit, vegetables, grains, and calories to store, which have been adapted into the above reference chart. 2 You know what your family likes to eat, and you may discover that your family consumes more fruits and vegetables than the chart suggests. A serving of fresh fruits and vegetables is approximately 4 ounces. However, different fruits and vegetables lose water at different rates. Refer to Chapter 9 to see how fresh fruits and vegetables transform into their dehydrated forms in order to get a more accurate idea of portion sizes.

CHAPTER 2: DEHYDRATING METHODS

Harness the Sun

Food drying by sunlight has been a common practice for centuries and is most effective in hot, dry climates. It is not advised for those who reside in colder, wetter northern climates. Even those living in the South are unable to achieve success due to the excessive humidity. The optimal temperature is between 90 and 100 degrees Fahrenheit, with relative humidity below 60 percent.

Create a series of drying racks from old picture frames by covering them with window screening or cotton sheeting if these conditions apply to your climate. Use staples to attach the screens to the bottom of the frames. Consider the food safety of the materials you are using and make appropriate preparations. The screens must be safe for contact with food, so avoid hardware cloth and other materials available at home improvement stores that are coated with galvanized metal. Choose instead stainless steel, fiberglass with a Teflon coating, or plastic. These materials will clean well and will not oxidize when exposed to sunlight.

Place the food you are drying on the screens and set the prepared frames in full sunlight for several days until the food is dry. Airflow is important for success. The trays can be stacked with wooden blocks between them to aid the process. Cover the food with cheesecloth to keep pests away during the drying time. Bring the racks in at night before the dew falls, or if there is excessive wind or it looks like it might rain. You don't want all your hard work to be undone.

For those that are living off-grid, solar drying may be your only option. Several plans can be found online for creating an enclosed solar box dehydrator. The enclosed-box drying method is less susceptible to humidity than regular solar methods and, compared with sun drying on racks, the temperature is higher and drying time is shorter. These appear to be relatively easy to make using salvaged materials around your home. Search "solar dehydrator box" or "solar dehydrator plans" in your favorite search engine for ideas.

In the Oven

Dehydrating in the oven is perhaps the most inefficient way to preserve your food because you need to keep your oven door open during the process. Oven drying takes two or three times longer than drying in a dehydrator and has a higher energy cost. While it does produce a safe and tasty product, the quality is different from food prepared in an electric dehydrator. Oven-dried food is more brittle and usually darker and less flavorful than food dried in a dehydrator. Don't let this deter you; an oven will work in a pinch if it is all you have. It requires little or no investment in equipment.

Test your oven temperature with a thermometer before you use it to dry food. Set the oven to the lowest temperature setting and prop open the door for one hour. The oven should maintain a temperature of between 130° to 150°F. If the oven does not maintain the temperature range, your finished product will begin to cook instead of dry. Conversely, if the temperature is too cool, you run the risk of food spoilage.

Using a Dehydrator

Years ago I purchased an old Ronco dehydrator at a garage sale for just a few bucks. It has 10 trays, no motor, and uses radiant bottom heat to dry the food. I thought I was in heaven. This machine is considered a dinosaur by today's fancy dehydrator standards, but I still have it and use it every year when I'm drying herbs. I love how quiet it is.

My next garage sale treasure was a Harvest Maid Dehydrator with a box of four extra trays. I have used that machine for years, creating all the things you read about in this book. It has an electric motor and blower at the base of the unit. Seriously, I've used these second-hand machines for at least 15 years. They are workhorses and prove that you don't need a fancy machine to have a prepared pantry.

Today's electric dehydrators make your pantry preservation even easier, and they run more efficiently than those old machines. In addition, many new machines have a timer to allow you to start and stop drying when it suits your schedule, and their 1000-watt heaters get the job done in record time. There are three basic dehydrator designs on the market today.

TYPES OF DEHYDRATORS

Dehydrators need to circulate air in order to do their job. This is accomplished by pushing air vertically through the machine, either from the bottom or the top, or by circulating air from the side horizontally.

Older model vertical airflow dehydrators have a heating element and fan located at the base of the unit, and the trays are stacked on top. This was the golden standard for years, and with a moving motor, it's a step up from my old Ronco machine. The one drawback to these old airflow machines is that the food does not dry evenly on the trays. The trays always need to be rotated from the top of the stack to the bottom to ensure each tray gets equal airflow. That can be a problem if you were hoping to load the machine and walk away until the food is dry.

In modern dehydrators, vertical airflow is accomplished by having a powerful motor at the top of the stack. This allows for a cleaner heating element and forces heated, pressurized air downward through the outer ring of the food trays. These machines are very efficient. At the same time, the circulating air moves horizontally across each tray and out through the bottom, and the air converges at the center for fast, even drying. I've found that with my Nesco Gardenmaster machine, there's no need to rotate trays—all the food dehydrates at the same time and it can handle up to 20 trays. You can efficiently dry a lot of food at one time.

Excalibur is the gold standard of horizontal airflow dehydrator units; it is also the most expensive. The heating element and fan are located in the back of the machine and provide horizontal airflow, which is said to reduce flavor mixing when you are dehydrating several different foods at one time. All trays receive equal heat distribution, and because cool air is drawn in, heated, and distributed evenly over each tray, the food dries faster and retains more nutrients, without tray rotation. If you are going to dry a lot of jerky, soup, or fruit leather, a dehydrator with horizontal airflow may be the best choice.

I now own five different dehydrators, including a Nesco Gardenmaster and an Excalibur 9-tray model. Each one, old and new, is regularly used for different drying purposes. You don't need a dehydrator to dry food, but it sure does make it easier and more efficient.

When you are drying large batches, it is helpful to have more than one dehydrator. The machine with bottom heat dries my herbs; it is the least precise of the machines and the one that needs tray rotation. It works well for herbs because they are not prone to spoiling, like some fruit or vegetables that need constant airflow. The Nesco Gardenmaster top-heat machine makes terrific work of fruit and vegetables, and I've found that there is very little tray rotation that needs to take place. It has digital time and heat instruments so I can schedule time in half-hour stages and adjust the temperature in 5°F increments. The Excalibur machine is square and is perhaps a more efficient use of tray space. With horizontal heating from the back, it makes excellent jerky and leathers.

Which one should you choose, horizontal or vertical airflow? It really is a personal preference. Any of the machines on the market today will dry food. I suggest you start with a machine that fits your budget and then expand to a large-capacity machine if you need to.

DEHYDRATOR BASICS

As a general rule, food should not be touching as it dries on dehydrator trays. This additional space aids with airflow and will help to dry your product fast and evenly. Also, juicy fruits like strawberries, mango, or watermelon will stick together when drying if they touch on the trays. The exception to this rule is leafy vegetables like cabbage, lettuce, spinach, or cilantro. They can be added to trays up to ½-inch thick, although you will need to reach in every few hours and stir the leaves.

If you have a machine with bottom heat, it is often necessary to aid your machine with air circulation by rotating the trays from top to bottom. Set a timer for halfway through the drying process and move the top tray to the bottom, shuffling each tray as you go. When finished, the original tray on the top will now be on the bottom of the stack. If you have a machine with horizontal airflow, rotate the trays 90 degrees halfway through the process. As you use your machine more often, you'll get to know its ins and outs and how much help it needs with airflow.

There are many variables in food dehydration. Humidity, methods of food handling, and different kinds of produce will change the quality of your dried food each time you make a batch. The only way to become an expert is to keep experimenting until you understand how each of the items you wish to store in your pantry will behave. Fortunately, dehydrating is a forgiving preservation method.

Microwave Drying

Microwave drying is not recommended for fruit, vegetables, and meat because of the uneven way they cook. All microwaves are designed to retain the moisture content in foods, not as a method of drying them. Also, fruits have high sugar content and will have a tendency to burn if they are overcooked in the microwave.

If you are determined to use your microwave for dehydrating, follow these rules:

1. Use the defrost setting (reduced power) to minimize the hardening effect that can happen when food is dried too quickly.
2. Cut food no more than ¼ inch thick.
3. Lay the product directly on the turnstile.
4. Dry in small batches.
5. Do not overlap food.
6. Turn the food every 15 minutes until it has dried to the consistency you are looking for.

Microwave drying is not a process where you can push the button and step away, unlike drying with an electric dehydrator. You must constantly monitor the batch to make sure the food does not get too dry, burn, and catch fire. And it will catch fire if you do not watch it continually!

For the best success, skip the fruit, and use the microwave to dehydrate only herbs or leafy greens. These contain a very minimal amount of moisture and are best suited for microwave drying. Place washed and towel-dried herbs on a paper towel or napkin and dry in 30-second increments until they reach the consistency you are looking for. See Chapter 8 about drying herbs for more information.

CHAPTER 3: BASIC DEHYDRATING TIPS

Learning to dehydrate gives you a tremendous variety of food that can be stored in your prepared pantry. Fortunately, there is room for creativity in the process. There is more than one way to prepare food for processing, but each fruit and vegetable is treated differently. This chapter will discuss small- and large-batch processing, how to pretreat food using blanching and oxidizing techniques, and how to store the food once you have it dried.

Keep these tips, applicable to all methods of dehydrating, in mind as you begin:

- **Cut pieces evenly.** Use a mandoline or salad chopper to achieve evenly cut pieces; this helps with faster drying times.
- **Clean your produce.** Thoroughly clean each piece of produce. This is especially important if you are not buying or growing organic.
- **Use fresh, ripe produce.** Choose fruit and vegetables at their peak freshness. Items that are underripe will not have a good flavor. Overripe fruit can still be used when making fruit leather.
- **Group similarly sized pieces on the same tray.** The size of the piece to be dehydrated is important; for even drying, keep all like sizes and thicknesses together on the trays.

Supplies Needed

BASIC SUPPLIES

One of the best things about dehydrating food is how simple it is. Only a few basic supplies are needed for success, and most of them are already in your kitchen.

- drying racks
- heat source (dehydrator, the sun, an oven)
- jars, for storage
- plastic fruit leather trays or plastic wrap
- pot, for blanching
- sharp knife
- slotted spoon
- cutting board
- strainer to wash produce

ADDITIONAL SUPPLIES

Once you have mastered dehydration, you will find ways to include dried food in all of your food preparations. After a while, I sought out time-saving items to expedite the process and have since added several other supplies to my "kit" for food dehydration.

Here are some additional tools that facilitate cutting, chopping, and pureeing. You may wish to acquire them as your budget permits:

- 100cc oxygen absorbers
- apple peeler/corer—once you use one, you'll never process an apple by hand again!
- blender or food processor
- canning funnels—handy for transferring dried items into jars
- food-grade buckets for long-term storage of all supplies
- mandoline slicer, to quickly give you uniform and specialty cuts for soft and hard vegetables
- Paraflexx trays
- salad shooter, for soft vegetables like zucchini and tomatoes
- vacuum sealer and bags
- vegetable brush, to scrub root vegetables clean
- vegetable peelers, to save your fingers from sharp knives

These extended supplies are not required, but they are useful if you are processing large quantities of food and want to extend the shelf life. Having them present can shorten lengthy tasks and allow you to process more food. Start with the least expensive items and buy more as your skills improve.

Dehydrating in Small Batches

You can afford to keep a dehydrator on your countertop at all times because they are so inexpensive to operate. They are ideal for preserving the remaining spinach or apples that will not be consumed before they begin to rot. In small batches, anything can be dehydrated. I recently purchased multiple bundles of cilantro for homemade salsa and discovered that I had two large handfuls leftover. Instead of making another batch of salsa or composting the cilantro, I cleaned the leaves, trimmed the stems, and processed two trays of the herb. This has been ground into a powder and will be used to flavor sauces and dips in the future. Use these tips to dehydrate food in small quantities.

- Cut the food into uniform sizes to aid with uniform drying times.
- Most dehydrators need proper airflow to do their job and work best with at least four trays. If you don't have four trays of food, alternate full and blank trays to make the required number.
- It's alright to have trays with different food items, but steer clear of mixing onion or garlic with other types of food; their flavors will taint the food on the other trays.

Dehydrating in Large Batches

When I am unable to grow enough of my own produce, I enjoy purchasing large quantities of in-season fruits and vegetables from the local farmers' market. This allows me to efficiently stock my pantry. Dehydrating a large quantity of food can take an entire day and requires some stamina to complete.

Produce growers have standardized the packaging of their goods, so if you want to buy fruit or vegetables in bulk from a local market, they will (often at a discount) sell it to you in 40-pound boxes. This is a large quantity of produce to wash, cut, prevent oxidation of, and place on dehydrating trays; therefore, it is important to do so efficiently. Here are some tips for dehydrating larger quantities of food.

- Make sure you have enough dehydrators to hold the produce. Borrow from friends if necessary.
- Set up a conditioning and packaging area, so dried food can get stored as soon as possible.
- Processing is easier if you break it into stations. Set up a cleaning station, cutting station, and blanching or oxidizing station to make the best use of your space.
- Consider purchasing tools to speed up the processing. Using a mandoline slicer or food processor will make the cutting job go faster and give you uniform pieces.
- Plan ahead and know which cuts you will be making. A 40-pound box of apples can be made into chips, diced for baking, or turned into applesauce and dried.
- Get help from friends and family. Teach the next generation how fun it is as they learn to dry their own food.

Blanching Vegetables for Dehydrating

Each vegetable has its own rule to follow prior to being placed in the freezer or dehydrator; you must be aware of these rules before deciding whether or not to break them. Some vegetables require blanching, others may require blanching, and others should be left alone.

When blanching vegetables, they are boiled or steamed for a few minutes and then cooled in ice water. Blanching time varies depending on the type of vegetable, but is typically between two and five minutes. This process halts the enzyme activity that leads to nutrient loss and texture change in frozen plants.

Vegetables that have been blanched can be placed directly onto dehydrator trays and processed for the appropriate amount of time.

No-blanch vegetables. Several vegetable varieties can be frozen or dried without blanching. These are my favorites because they are so convenient to store! They can be washed, halved, quartered, or chopped, then dried with a towel and placed directly in the dehydrator. Washing mushrooms will result in discoloration. Instead, use a towel to clean the mushrooms. Leave the stems of herbs and leafy greens (such as parsley, cilantro, and spinach) several inches long. Wash by swishing in cold water, then drying with a towel.

Maybe-blanch vegetables. Some crops may need to be blanched. These typically require minimal blanching in boiling water, and you may find great success by omitting it altogether. When rehydrated, the texture of these foods remains suitable for soups, stews, and casseroles. These have a shelf life of up to one year, so it is best to only prepare what you will use within that time frame and to rotate your supplies frequently.

The key to skipping the blanching step for these vegetables lies in their preparation prior to processing. If the pieces are small enough, the step can typically be skipped. These vegetables must be thoroughly cleaned, chopped, and dried with a towel to remove excess moisture.

The process of dehydration is straightforward. Place the vegetables in a single layer on the dehydrator sheets and process them according to their individual temperatures and processing times. After drying, place in canning jars and store in a cool, dark location.

Always-blanch vegetables. Before you can freeze or dehydrate certain vegetables, you must always blanch them first. You should only consume vegetables in pristine condition.

SET UP A BLANCHING STATION

If you dislike blanching vegetables as much as I do, consider creating a blanching station to expedite the process. Create a production line from your stovetop to your sink.

For removing the vegetables from the stockpot, you will require a stockpot, several clean towels, cold water, a bag of ice, and a sieve.

1. Bring the water in a stockpot to a rolling boil.
2. Fill a kitchen sink or a bathtub insert with ice and cold water.
3. Place a small amount of vegetables in the boiling water for the specified amount of time, then transfer them to the cold water bath using a sieve.
4. Remove the blanched vegetables from the water and place them on a kitchen towel to dry after they have cooled.
5. Method for dehydration on dehydrator trays.

Fruit Pretreatments to Prevent Oxidization

Some fruits become brown when exposed to the air for too long. Among them are apples, bananas, pears, and peaches, among others. Pretreatment of the fruit prior to drying will prevent discoloration and may help preserve nutrients and texture. This step is optional, and if you choose to omit it, the final product will still be delicious. Consider that if you skip pretreatments, the fruit may not look how your family expects it to, and they may be less inclined to consume it.

Fruit may undergo two types of pretreatments: dipping in a solution and blanching in steam.

FRUIT DIPPING

There is room for individual interpretation when dehydrating fruit, as dehydration is not an exact science. Choose between honey dip, lemon juice, and ascorbic acid. I would suggest tasting fruit with each type of dip and then preparing a batch with none. You may discover that the entire procedure is unimportant to your family.

Ascorbic acid or citric acid (vitamin C) dip. You can find vitamin C and ascorbic acid in the pharmacy or in the canning section of your local supermarket. This method does not leave the fruit with an aftertaste.

To create the remedy: Combine two tablespoons of powder and one quart of water. Soak the fruit for two to three minutes in small batches. Before placing on dehydrator trays, remove with a slotted spoon and let dry.

Fruit juice dip. Citric acid occurs naturally in pineapple, lemon, and lime, and their juice makes an excellent pretreatment, although it is less effective than ascorbic acid. The fruit may acquire a slight flavor from dipping in juice.

To create the remedy: Mix 1 cup of juice with 1 quart of warm water, and soak small batches of fruit for 10 minutes. Before placing on dehydrator trays, remove with a slotted spoon and let dry.

Honey dip. If you choose a honey dip, the fruit will be sweeter and contain more calories. This will achieve the consistency of dehydrated fruit purchased from a store, which your children may prefer.

To create the remedy: Dissolve one cup of sugar in three cups of hot water. Allow the mixture to cool until it is barely warm, then stir in 1 cup honey. Before placing fruit on dehydrator sheets, dunk it in the mixture in small batches, remove it with a slotted spoon, and drain it thoroughly. Consider parchment paper or non-stick dehydrator tray covers, as this fruit will adhere to your trays.

BLANCHING

Steam-boiling. The majority of fruits are too delicate to boil and retain their shape. Instead, to prevent oxidation, steam the fruit pieces in small batches for one minute, then dip them in ice water and drain well before placing them on trays.

Boil blanching. Certain fruits must be completely blanched prior to dehydration, which improves the texture and drying time of the final product. These include plums, apricots, blueberries, cranberries, gooseberries, currants, and grapes (raisins) (prunes). Simply place these fruits in a colander, dip them in boiling water for 30 seconds, cool them in ice water, and drain them.

Before beginning the dehydrating process, your fruit must be as dry as possible after being dipped in these pretreatment solutions. If you add wet fruit to the trays, the drying time for each batch will increase significantly.

Food Touching on Trays

There are significant differences between drying herbs, fruits, and vegetables. You may wonder whether fresh items can touch while drying on the tray. Observe these general guidelines:

Herbs and leafy greens. On the drying trays, piles of herbs and leafy greens can be placed. Their low water content will prevent them from adhering, and they will dry quickly. Pick out the dried leaves each hour, combine the remaining leaves, and continue processing until the entire batch is complete.

Vegetables. On drying trays, most vegetables can be placed close together and even touch. If the proper drying temperature of 125 to 135 degrees Fahrenheit is used, they will reduce in size relatively quickly and leave sufficient space for airflow. They will not adhere when they dry. Again, remove dried pieces every few hours and continue drying the remainder.

Fruits. Due to the high sugar content of most fruits, they should be spread out in a single layer on drying trays without touching. Any pieces that touch will dry as a single unit and may even adhere to the tray as they dry. Utilize tray covers or parchment paper to prevent sticking, and rotate the food every few hours.

Conditioning the Finished Product

Properly dried fruit will have a 20 percent moisture content. We use a conditioning process to equalize the moisture level in the final product because those who produce food at home lack a method for measuring the moisture content. Conditioning ensures that all fruit pieces have dried evenly and prevents the growth of mold and bacteria during storage. This must be completed prior to packaging for long-term storage.

1. Take the cooled, dried fruit and loosely pack it into glass preserving jars. Ensure there is sufficient space for movement when shaking the jar.
2. The jar must be tightly sealed and shaken daily for seven days.
3. Check for condensation of moisture. Return wet items to the dehydrator to continue

drying.
4. Once the process has been completed, continue with standard packaging. Instructions are available in Chapter 5.
5. Pieces that have begun to develop mold must be discarded; they cannot be saved.

General Rehydrating Techniques

Food that has been dehydrated is typically hard, brittle, and unappealing in appearance. You'll be surprised at how quickly and completely the food returns to its original shape after reintroducing water. Not all dehydrated food items can be rehydrated using these techniques. Most fruits are dried and consumed as snacks. Instead of being rehydrated, some vegetables are eaten as chips or incorporated into powdered spice blends.

SOAK

Soaking is both the simplest and slowest method for rehydrating food. Place a measured amount of dried food in a bowl and soak it in an equal amount of water for 10 to 30 minutes, depending on the desired texture. Pour off any excess liquid that has not been absorbed by the food.

Fruit must be submerged in cool water. It is possible to soak vegetables in cool, warm, or even boiling water. Consider soaking the ingredients in juice or broth for a flavor variation, and then instead of pouring off the extra liquid, incorporating it directly into the recipe.

Be sure to adhere to the specific rehydration requirements outlined in Chapter 9 for each item.

As a general rule, you can soak food on the kitchen counter for up to an hour if you will be doing so. If you are preparing things early in the day and intend to use the food for dinner, place the soaking bowl in the refrigerator. It will only absorb as much liquid as it needs, and the excess can be poured away. Refrigeration prevents deterioration and contamination. Never leave food on the counter for more than two hours without refrigeration.

SPRAY

Occasionally, spraying delicate fruit with water is all that is required to restore its original shape. Place the food in a shallow bowl or on a plate and spray the food until water droplets form. Permit the water to absorb, and continue spraying until the fruit regains its original form. Maintain a spray bottle in the kitchen and give this method a try.

SIMMER OR COOK

I like to add dehydrated vegetables to my morning scrambled eggs. Instead of rehydrating everything prior to use, I place everything in a skillet with just enough water to cover and simmer for five minutes. Once the water has evaporated, they will have expanded, and I will add the eggs.

Some foods can be added to a recipe without being rehydrated. You can add dried corn, beans, broccoli, cauliflower, or peas directly to the pot when making soup, then add additional broth or water to maintain the desired consistency.

Record Keeping

When you are learning how to dehydrate different types of food for the first time, or if it has been a while since you last did so, it is helpful to be able to refer back to the method you used previously. The key to success is maintaining accurate records. It will enhance your dehydrating techniques and save you a great deal of trial and error the next time you need to dry something. This can be accomplished using a card file or an electronic spreadsheet.

Here are some things you may wish to monitor:
- Special conditioning
- Use-by date
- Date dried
- Quantity dried (e.g., 12 apples)
- Weight of produce before drying (e.g., 6 pounds)
- Weight of produce after drying (e.g., 2 pounds)
- Humidity percent on day of drying
- Drying temperature
- Drying time
- Packaging used
- Preparation method, including:
    - Quantity and type of spices used
    - Cut used (julienne, fry cut, crinkle cut, waffle cut, diced, etc.)
    - Cut thickness
    - Blanching or oxidizing process used
- Additional notes: how it turned out, what you would change next time

CHAPTER 4: FOOD SAFETY AND HYGIENE

Because dehydration is a relatively straightforward process, you may be tempted to begin without taking safety precautions into account. How difficult can it be, after all, to dehydrate an apple? This is the benefit of dehydrating food at home. It is simple to take the necessary precautions to ensure that your food is safe to consume. You will quickly have a fully stocked pantry if you select the highest-quality produce, clean it thoroughly, ensure that it is properly conditioned for storage, and avoid a few problematic items.

Select the Best Produce

Fresh fruits and vegetables will yield the best outcomes. If you can purchase fruits and vegetables from a farmer's market or grow them yourself, that is preferable.

Fruit. Begin by selecting firm, flavorful fruit at its peak of ripeness. Handle it with care to prevent bruising, and prepare it as soon as possible after bringing it home. If some of the fruit is bruised or overripe by the time you reach it, process it into fruit leather.

Vegetables. When vegetables are fresh, tender, and ripe, they are ready to be dehydrated. As soon as possible after harvesting, process them. Vegetables that are immature will have poor color and flavor, and rehydration will not restore their fresh flavor. Avoid vegetables that are overripe, as they may become fibrous. As with fruit, overripe vegetables can be transformed into leather, which can be used as a thickener and flavoring agent in soup.

Clean Fruit and Vegetables

No mother would want to introduce chemicals and pesticides into their children's daily diets, so every mother would strive to provide her family with only the freshest, organic produce. Unfortunately, purchasing organic produce can be difficult on the wallet. You may also have access to large quantities of fresh fruits and vegetables that are not organic. Thankfully, there is a method for cleaning produce that has been sprayed with chemicals. If you are diligent, you can remove more than 95 percent of pesticides from the surface.

This technique was first taught to me by Daisy Luther on her blog The Organic Prepper. Adapted from her book, The Prepper's Canning Guide.

Use this method to thoroughly clean all of your fruits and vegetables before dehydrating them. In addition to removing pesticides and traces of fertilizer, it also eliminates dirt. It may require an additional step, but it's worthwhile. The best part is that you already have these ingredients on hand.

1. Pour one cup of baking soda and one squirt of natural dish soap into a sink or bathtub filled with hot water. For softer produce, such as berries, use cool water.
2. Soak the produce for approximately twenty minutes in the solution. There may be an alarming white film of slime on the surface of the water. That indicates that the method is effective and the vegetables are being cleaned.
3. Rinse the produce and then empty the sink. Produce that is robust can be rinsed in a

steady stream of water. For delicate produce, scrub a clean sink or bathtub, fill it with cool, fresh water, and swish the produce in the clean water.

4. Scrub the exterior of thick-skinned, firm produce such as apples with a cloth. Let delicate produce drain in a colander.
5. If a film remains or the rinse water is cloudy, clean the sink with white vinegar and repeat the process.

LEAFY GREENS WASH

According to the CDC, leafy greens such as lettuce, spinach, and cilantro can be difficult to clean thoroughly and are more likely to be contaminated with E. coli bacteria. This natural cleanser was found to eliminate 98% of bacteria on produce. It is simple to make and uses ingredients from your pantry.

In a bowl or shallow tub, combine 3 cups of cool water and 1 cup of white vinegar that has been distilled. Soak your greens in the bowl for approximately two minutes, and then rinse them thoroughly.

What Not to Dehydrate

Because dehydration is so simple, you may be tempted to dehydrate all of your favorite foods. However, there are a few items that are not recommended due to safety concerns. Others are so time-consuming to process that it is preferable to purchase them from professionals rather than attempting them yourself. In general, it is preferable to err on the side of caution when handling these items.

Eggs. There are numerous online preppers who provide instructions for dehydrating eggs. I am not among them. In order to prevent salmonella poisoning, raw eggs must be stored at temperatures below 45°F. Therefore, in my opinion, raw eggs should not be left on a dehydrator tray for 10 to 12 hours while they are being processed.

Other bloggers prepare their eggs by cooking, drying, and then powdering them. I've heard that these eggs have a consistency problem and that they will never rehydrate properly without becoming grainy. Professionals are your best bet for purchasing egg powder, in my opinion. A #10 container will cost approximately $35 and will be an excellent investment. These eggs will supply you with baking eggs for an entire year, and you will never have to worry about making your family sick.

Foods high in fat. These items are not suitable for dehydration. High-fat foods typically do not dry well and are susceptible to spoilage. These items, like eggs, are dehydrated or freeze-dried by professionals and readily available for online purchase. Do not undertake the task yourself. Avoid butter, cheese, and avocado, which are all high in fat content.

Meat and fish. Always exercise extreme caution when dehydrating meat. Why take up valuable storage space when dried meats (including jerky) should be stored in the refrigerator or freezer? You will have greater success preserving meat and fish using the pressure canning method. They will last a year, are completely shelf stable, and can be poured directly from the jar for a quick meal.

Only jerky is an exception. Choose a raw meat cut that is as fat-free as possible, and dry or brine cure it for 6 to 12 hours. For longer shelf life, the finished product can be stored in vacuum-sealed bags. In Chapter 7, we'll discuss the specifics of making your own jerky.

Milk. Milk is difficult to contain within dehydrator trays, and the entire process is typically messy. In reality, the time required to obtain a small quantity of powdered milk is not worth it in the long run. In the end, it is mostly water. It is a more efficient use of money and time to purchase whole milk powder from professionals.

Even if a food is on a do-not-dehydrate list, that does not mean it cannot be dehydrated; rather, the time, effort, potential risk, and lack of long-term storage options make it impractical. Focus on the rapid success of dehydrating fruits and vegetables, and learn how to make jerky, if you wish to construct a long-term pantry. They will construct your pantry quickly.

The Effects of Light, Oxygen, Heat, and Humidity on Dried Food

I currently reside in Central Texas in the South, but I am originally from the North. The majority of Northerners won't have to deal with humidity for the majority of the year, but if you live in the South, it can be a problem for months. There are special considerations for dehydrating food in a humid climate because the humid season tends to coincide with harvest season.

According to the article "Drying Food" published by the University of Illinois, College of Agriculture, the rate of dehydration will increase as temperature and humidity decrease. Humid air inhibits evaporation. Consider this if you intend to dry food during hot, humid summer days." [3]

Dehydration facilitates the loss of moisture from food via evaporation. In the absence of adequate ventilation, the humid air within a dehydrator quickly absorbs as much moisture as it can hold, rendering drying impossible. For this reason, ensure that your food dryer has adequate ventilation. If there is sufficient airflow, the food will dry quicker and use less energy.

If you live in a humid environment, you will also need to quickly package your dried produce. If you leave your dried tomatoes on the counter in a humid home overnight, you will need to reprocess them the following day. Consider dehydrated food as a sponge that loves to absorb liquid and moisture. It can readily absorb atmospheric moisture, becoming less dry and susceptible to mold. In Chapter 5, we will discuss how to avoid this with packaging and storage.

The three elements most likely to reduce the shelf life of dehydrated foods are light, heat, and oxygen. Here are some general guidelines:

- Check dried foods regularly during storage to see if they are still dry. Glass containers work well for this; moisture that collects on the sides is easy to see.
- Discard all food that has developed an off smell or shows signs of mold.
- Displaying canning jars full of processed food on an open shelf looks pretty, but it is a surefire way to undermine all the hard work you've done. Always keep your food in a cool, dark, dry cabinet to ensure the longest shelf life.
- Storage temperature helps determine the length of storage. With proper packaging, most dried food can be stored for one year at 60°F and six months at 80°F.
- Pack foods in amounts that can be used all at once. Every time you open a package, you introduce moisture and air that can lower the quality of the food.
- If the dehydrated food shows signs of moisture and the food has not spoiled, you can use it immediately, or reprocess and repackage it.

One final consideration must be made when drying food. It is known as "case hardening." You may be tempted to increase the dehydrator's temperature in order to quickly remove moisture and complete the task. In any case, it stands to reason that removing moisture from food more rapidly will require less energy, correct? Unfortunately, that is not how it works. If the food is dried too quickly, the outermost cells will lose water more quickly than the innermost cells. The surface will harden, preventing moisture from the interior from escaping, and drying will take even longer. And if you increase the heat too much, you will cook the food rather than dehydrate it.

Using Frozen Vegetables

Consider purchasing frozen vegetables for dehydration if you do not have access to a large garden or farmer's market. These vegetables are frequently available in large quantities, making them an economical option. Keep an eye out for grocery coupons to save even more money.

The blanching of frozen vegetables was performed by the processor prior to freezing. All frozen vegetables can be placed directly on the food dehydrator trays without any additional preparation, which is a quick win for your pantry. You need not even defrost them. Simply throw the bag a few times against the countertop to break up any frozen clumps. Place any remaining ice on a kitchen towel or paper towel and rub vigorously to remove it. The towel will absorb the ice crystals, and the product will be ready for dehydration. The processing time ranges between 6 and 16 hours. Follow the dehydrating times specified for each vegetable in Chapter 9's description.

These frozen vegetables dehydrate effectively:

- Corn
- Okra
- Peas
- Broccoli
- Carrots
- Cauliflower
- Vegetable mix (baby lima beans, carrots, corn, green beans, peas)

A word of caution: search for frozen vegetables in their most natural state. Bags containing added sauce or oil are incompatible with dehydration and should not be used. Additionally, you will find that some producers add sugar to their vegetables. Examine the ingredients carefully and decide if this fits into your food storage plans.

Using Frozen Fruit

Purchasing large bags of frozen fruit to dehydrate is a fantastic way to save freezer space and have almost-fresh fruit. This is an effective method for preserving fruit that you cannot grow yourself. These bags are frequently on sale at the local grocery store.

There is no need to pre-treat the fruit because it has already been blanched and oxidized by the commercial packaging. Start with a bag of frozen fruit, spread it evenly on your dehydrator trays, and set the temperature to 125 to 130 degrees Fahrenheit. Wetness-free for six to eight hours. If you can set it up before bed, they will be completely dry when you wake up in the morning.

Frozen fruit has a tendency to drip inside the dehydrator as it dries; therefore, if you are dehydrating more than one type of fruit, you should place an additional Paraflexx sheet or plastic fruit leather tray beneath each type of fruit. This will prevent strawberry juice from dripping onto the pineapple chunks below.

These frozen fruits dehydrate effectively:
- Peaches
- Pineapple
- Blueberries
- Mangoes
- Strawberries

Buying Large Quantities of Produce

My strategy for food storage is based on bulk purchases. What this actually means is that I seek out items on sale and buy them in bulk. I, too, wait until the appropriate time to make such purchases.

Consider fresh fruits and vegetables as an illustration. I am aware that the blueberry season runs from June to August. I am also aware that when blueberries become available in June at grocery stores and farmers markets, they will be expensive. Everyone desires fresh blueberries for their recipes, and the vendor knows they can charge a premium price—and that we will likely pay it—because they are, after all, fresh blueberries.

By mid-August, the market will be saturated, and fresh blueberries will no longer be in high demand. This is when the bulk purchaser is rewarded for their patience. The market will be flooded with berries that farmers are attempting to remove from their fields, and you guessed it: they will reduce their prices to entice you to buy. Now that the price is so low, you can purchase blueberries in bulk and store them for the remainder of the year. If you live close to a blueberry farm and are willing to attend a pick-your-own event, you will receive an even better price.

Don't overlook local independent fruit stand businesses when purchasing in bulk. They frequently sell in bulk and provide a discount. Buying by the case or tray is typically less expensive. You can also check out warehouse clubs such as Costco or Sam's Club, or ask your local grocery store if they offer discounts for bulk purchases.

There is always strength in numbers, and buying in bulk may be your solution. If you can join forces with like-minded individuals to make purchases, you will receive an even better price. Here are some examples:
- Join a CSA and support a local farmer.
- Look for local food co-ops and see what they have to offer. These might be the best places to purchase dry goods like flour, grains, and beans.
- See if there is a Meetup group in your area that is purchasing in bulk.

Still stumped? Make your own organization. You must have like-minded friends! Conduct a Facebook poll to determine which of your friends within a 20-mile radius are interested in food storage cost savings. Once the core group has been assembled, brainstorm items that need to be purchased and assign the group the task of finding deals.

PURCHASE A BUSHEL, BAG, BOX, OR FLAT

Not everyone has the time, space, or desire to cultivate a large garden, and in reality, no one can grow everything their family needs to eat. For instance, bananas are difficult to cultivate in the majority of the world. There is an entire grassroots movement surrounding eating locally, but we will not discuss its benefits in this book. We are fortunate to be able to purchase any fruit or vegetable from a local farmer, grocery store, or big box store in the majority of the world.

When I lived outside of Portland, Oregon, I frequented Justy's Produce and Flowers, a local produce stand. I miss the helpful service and the ability to purchase fresh food in bulk at that establishment, which I adore. I have not yet discovered anything comparable in Central Texas. I believe that every community should have a helpful produce guy (or gal) who can locate a box of pickling cucumbers or Roma tomatoes at a great price. If you know which fruits and vegetables are in season each month and the standard box size for buying in bulk, you can save money and have enough for storage.

Packaging standards. There are specific industry packaging size and weight requirements for the wholesale sale of specific crops. This is done to ensure that everyone in the industry speaks the same packaging language and understands what is being bought and sold. As a result of the fact that each crop has unique handling requirements, the industry utilizes boxes, cartons, lugs, crates, flats, bags, sacks, and bulk bins of varying sizes. The two most common units of measurement are bushels and pecks. A bushel of produce contains 8 gallons (32 quarts) and is equivalent to 4 pecks and 2,150 cubic inches. Here are some additional common packaging standards you should be aware of. 4

- *Flats* hold 12 (1-pint) boxes
- *Lugs* are shallow containers, usually wood, that vary in size
- *Sacks* are 50 or 100 pounds of dry vegetables or commodities like potato, onion, beans, and rice
- *Bags* are paper and polyethylene, often with handles, and hold ¼ peck to ½ bushel
- *Baskets* are made of wood, and hold anywhere between ¼ peck and 1 bushel
- *Boxes, cartons, or hampers* hold anywhere from ½ peck to 1 bushel
- *Trays* are used for berries and are made of corrugated paper. They hold either 6 to 8 quarts or 10 to 15 pounds

Grade and size standards. Moreover, the U.S. Department of Agriculture or individual states determine the grade and size of packaging for each crop of produce. The majority of the fresh produce sold in grocery stores is U.S. Grade No. 1 or better. The difference between No. 1 and lower grades is frequently minimal and relates to the product's appearance, not its flavor. These products below No. 1 are frequently sold to institutions and businesses that will transform them into finished goods.

Justy first taught me about the grading system at his produce stand, when I requested a box of pickling cucumbers and he inquired whether U.S. No. 2 pickles were acceptable. He explained that they would be firm, fresh, and disease-free, but their diameter and color would be irregular. The size and hue of cucumbers are irrelevant to my pickling endeavors, so I placed my order. The price was drastically reduced.

The USDA publishes grading specifications for all fruits and vegetables sold in the United States (visit the links in the footnotes to see the standards for individual fruit and vegetables). Apples, for instance, are sold in five distinct grades:

- U.S. No. 1
- U.S. No. 1 Hail
- U.S. Extra Fancy

- U.S. Fancy
- U.S. Utility

Why should you, as a home preserver, be familiar with these grade standards? Because you are also transforming these apples into a finished product, and because you now speak the language, you can purchase these lower-quality apples at a substantial discount. The distinction between U.S. No. 1 and U.S. No. 1 Hail has no effect on your applesauce: "U.S. No. 1 Hail" refers to apples that meet the requirements for U.S. No. 1 grade, with the exception that hail marks where the skin has not been broken, as well as well-healed hail marks where the skin has been broken, are permitted, as long as the apples are reasonably well formed.

You need only ask your grocer or produce vendor for these grades. You can save a lot of money by purchasing in this manner.

CHAPTER 5: STORING YOUR DEHYDRATED FOOD

The concept of a stocked pantry is central to my preparedness plan, and dehydrated foods play a significant role. Once you've mastered dehydrating your own food, you'll need to learn how to properly store it so that it remains edible for years.

Necessary Equipment

These essential items will prolong the shelf-stability of dried foods. The majority of our pantry storage is conducted with canning jars. They are readily available, simple to store, and compatible with all the food preservation techniques you will be employing.

Storage containers create a naturally airtight environment for food. Remove the oxygen from the storage container to increase the shelf life. This is achieved by using oxygen absorbers. By removing oxygen and replacing it with nitrogen, you can protect your food from insect damage and maintain its quality. The iron powder in oxygen-absorbing packets reacts with the oxygen in your container, causing the powder to rust. They pose no threat to your food.

Depending on the size of your storage container, you can purchase oxygen absorbers in a variety of sizes. One 100cc oxygen absorber per quart canning jar and one 300cc oxygen absorber (or three 100cc absorbers) per gallon of product are required. You can purchase larger, 2000cc oxygen absorbers for storing 5- or 6-gallon buckets.

Additionally, you can consider purchasing a vacuum sealer with a jar attachment. I use a vacuum sealer by FoodSaver. When using canning jars, these oxygen absorbers can be used instead of the 100cc oxygen absorbers. A vacuum sealer is advantageous, but not required.

We store all of our long-term supplies, both edible and non-edible, in food-grade buckets. Look for plastics with or imprinted on them. Obtain these from ULine.com, Wal-Mart, Amazon.com, or a nearby bakery or ice cream parlor.

For both long- and short-term storage, plastic freezer bags with zip-tops are advised. They are more airtight and airtight than standard storage bags.

Finally, foil coated with plastic Mylar pouches can be used as an alternative to plastic freezer bags, but this is the most costly method of storage. These durable bags are used with oxygen absorbers to remove air and light from dried foods.

Short-Term Vs. Long-Term Pantry

We maintain both short-term and long-term pantry items in our home.

Items of limited duration The items in our short-term pantry will be consumed within the next six months. These pantry items will have a shorter shelf life due to repeated exposure to light, heat, and humidity.

Bread and pancake mixes, as well as other items with leavening, crackers, bars with dried fruit and nuts, quart-size containers of the most common dehydrated fruits and vegetables, and canned food and spices could be included in a short-term pantry.

When we package our own food items, we store them in mason jars, food-grade plastic jars, or plastic zip-top bags. It is essential to keep your short-term pantry organized, so you always know what's inside.

Linda Loosli of Food Storage Moms has a resourceful method for expanding a small pantry. She suggests that by adding a few extra shelves to a small pantry, you can gain up to 50 percent more storage space, depending on how your cabinets are constructed. Her system also includes large and small pails filled with flour and sugar for daily baking, which she replenishes as necessary. Visit http://www.foodstoragemoms.com/2013/10/small-pantry for more information.

Long-term items. It is possible to store home-processed food for two to five years if the oxygen component is eliminated. I accomplish this by vacuum-packaging dry foods with a FoodSaver machine and placing them in plastic buckets with oxygen absorbers.

This is the procedure. Once your fruits or vegetables are completely dried and properly conditioned (see page 25), it is time to package them for storage. Divide the food into smaller portions (possibly six meals) and place them in an oxygen-free FoodSaver bag. If you do not have a FoodSaver, use 1-gallon freezer bags with zip-top closures, remove as much air as possible, and add one 300cc oxygen absorber per gallon bag. If the item has sharp edges (such as dried carrots), I additionally wrap it in plastic wrap to soften them. Be sure to label each of these smaller containers with the product's name and the date it was dehydrated so that you can rotate them appropriately.

After placing a 2000cc oxygen absorber in the bottom of a 5-gallon bucket, I begin layering smaller packaged items on top. You should move quickly to complete this task. Once exposed to air for 5 to 10 minutes, an oxygen absorber begins to lose its effectiveness. Label the exterior of the plastic bucket with its contents and the date it was sealed once it has been sealed.

The smaller packages of items are kept in our extended pantry and moved as needed to the short-term pantry. It is safe to remove packages from 5-gallon buckets as long as the buckets are promptly resealed.

We also purchase dehydrated vegetables, milk, and beans in #10 cans from ProvidentLiving.org in addition to storing the food we dehydrate. Professionally processed dried foods typically have a 20 to 30-year shelf life. At the time of writing, a can of diced onions weighing 2.4 pounds cost $9. It would require almost 10 pounds of onions, untold hours, and many tears for me to dry that many onions. Since the prices are very reasonable, I purchase my onions and carrots here rather than drying them myself.

Keeping Inventory

Without some sort of inventory system, it is difficult to keep track of what you have on hand. It becomes even more difficult if you live in a small home and store your belongings in unconventional places, such as under beds or in closets. It is essential to keep track of every item and where it is stored in order to prevent food waste.

This tracking system can be as straightforward as a yellow pad, as complex as an Excel spreadsheet, or as advanced as an online food storage tracker such as Home Food Storage by Long Term Glass Wares, LLC.

I can honestly say that I have tried nearly every inventory management technique available on the market today, and it is difficult to keep my inventory list current. The issue is that you must convince your family to track the food as well, or they will remove food and disrupt your system. In order to maintain an accurate inventory, you may find that you are the only person permitted to "check out" food from the long-term areas.

Rotating Your Food

Food rotation is a requirement of basic pantry protocols. First-in, first-out (FIFO) is the optimal method for maintaining a rotation of fresh foods. Rotating food FIFO means that each package of food is dated, and the oldest item is always stored in the front of the cabinet so that it can be consumed first. When new items are added to storage, the back of the cabinet is where they are placed.

There are numerous creative ways to organize your shelves for FIFO storage, and a rotating storage shelf may be the solution you seek. Internet search for DIY building plans Ultimately, the most important thing to remember when rotating food is to regularly prepare the items in your pantry. If you are preparing soups, stews, and chili with dehydrated ingredients rather than fresh ones, you will always use the stock you have on hand.

By labeling short-term and long-term storage containers with their contents and the date they were dried, you can keep track of your supply, rotate it as necessary, and prevent wasting the food that you spent so much time and money preparing.

CHAPTER 6: FRUIT AND VEGETABLE LEATHERS

Fruit leathers and fruit rolls are a favorite among both children and adults. When fruit becomes too ripe for other drying methods, they are a fantastic way to preserve small quantities of fruit. It is a delicacy that no one can refuse. You may use whatever fruit you have available. There are two fundamental preparation methods for fruit leather: uncooked and cooked.

In fruit leather recipes, sugar and honey are interchangeable ingredients. Honey will produce a slightly stickier and more flavorful roll. Consider using pure maple syrup to alter the flavor. In order to ensure that no sugar granules remain in the final product, it is best to make simple syrup before using sugar. Sugar will make the final product slightly more brittle.

Dehydrator Trays Liners for Making Leather

A standard dehydrator tray will not trap the pureed fruit used to make fruit leather. Most commercial dehydrators include one or two plastic fruit roll sheets for this specific purpose. These are constructed from a rigid plastic with a slight outer lip that prevents food from falling off the tray. Even if you acquired your machine secondhand, it is simple to find replacement trays online. If you make a substantial amount of fruit leather, you may wish to purchase sufficient liners for each tray.

Using a round machine to create leather is not the most efficient method, so I prefer to use the square Excalibur machine. Their non-stick dehydrator sheets work exceptionally well and are simple to clean.

It is not necessary to purchase an expensive lining for your leather; parchment paper or plastic wrap, cut to the size of your dehydrator trays, can be used instead. If you intend to create leather on circular trays, be sure to leave the center section uncovered, as this is where airflow occurs during the drying process. The use of foil and wax paper is inappropriate for this project.

General Instructions for Uncooked Fruit Leather

1. Completely wash the fruit. Use the cleaning method on page 28 to remove as much dirt and pesticide as possible from non-organic fruit.
2. Remove large stones and seeds. The removal of seeds from small-seeded fruits such as strawberries, blackberries, and raspberries is a matter of personal preference. This is most effectively achieved by blending the berries into a pulp and then straining the pulp through a fine mesh strainer. The pulp will pass through while the seeds are captured.
3. Peel the fruit and remove the typically unpalatable rough skins (melon, citrus). I prefer to leave the skins on my fruit whenever possible, as there are numerous nutrients in the skin.
4. The fruit should be cut into medium-sized pieces and placed in a blender or food

processor. Add citrus or ascorbic acid if you are concerned about fruit oxidation (see page 24). The fruit is blended into a thick puree.

5. If the puree is excessively juicy, strain it through a fine mesh strainer until it has the consistency of pudding. This is entirely subjective, so do not be afraid to experiment. You will discover the appropriate consistency for your machine and the fruit being used. If the mixture is too thick, add water in increments of 1 teaspoon until the desired consistency is reached.

6. As desired, add honey or sugar to the mixture. Add half a teaspoon of any spice per four cups of fruit puree.

7. Prepare your drying trays and fill them to within an inch of the edge with fruit puree. Using a ladle, scoop and evenly distribute the puree on the tray. The thickness should not exceed 14 inch, or the drying time will be affected. Therefore, the outer edges of the tray should be thicker than the interior. Using a ladle, redistribute the puree as desired by stirring it.

8. Dry at 125 degrees Fahrenheit for six to eight hours until leather is tacky. After it has dried, it will be translucent and slightly tacky. It will peel away from the plastic wrap or dehydrator sheet with ease. It's best to remove it while warm.

General Instructions for Cooked Fruit Leather

Occasionally, fruit should be cooked before being pureed. Before placing the fruit in the dehydrator, simmering it reduces the moisture content and concentrates the flavor. Certain fruits, such as rhubarb and cranberries, are always cooked before consumption and would not taste good in a puree if this step were skipped. Other fruits, such as apples, pears, coconuts, cherries, and blueberries, require softening prior to achieving a puree consistency.

1. Prepare the fruit according to steps 1, 2, and 3 beginning on page 38.

2. The fruit is cooked in a saucepan. Using a fork, assist the fruit in breaking down as it cooks by mashing it.

3. If desired, add ascorbic acid to prevent oxidation and honey or sugar to taste.

4. The fruit is blended into a thick puree.

5. Continue with steps 5 through 8 from the preceding instructions.

Utilize your finished fruit leathers in inventive ways. They may be rolled and consumed as-is, or rehydrated and utilized in pie fillings and dessert toppings. Blend five portions of water with one portion of leather to create a beverage.

How to Store Fruit Leather

When fruit leather is still slightly warm, it is easiest to manipulate. If it has completely cooled, reheat it in the dehydrator for five minutes. After the leather is dry and free of sticky residue, it can be stored in a variety of ways.

1. Place a sheet of leather on parchment paper or plastic wrap and roll it into a scroll shape. Cut the scroll into 1-inch segments using kitchen shears. To create bite-sized pieces, cut the sections into 1-inch squares. If you choose not to use paper, you can still roll the fruit leather, but it may need to be coated to prevent sticking. It is possible to dust it

with cornstarch or arrowroot powder. Neither of these will affect the finished product's flavor.

2. Place your cut rolls in plastic freezer bags or an airtight canning jar in a cool, dry location. Large quantities can be stored in the freezer or refrigerator for long-term preservation. A portion is stored in a jar in the pantry alongside a 100cc oxygen absorber.

What Can Go Wrong

Fruit leather that has been properly dehydrated will be translucent and slightly tacky to the touch. It will peel away from the plastic wrap or dehydrator sheet with ease. However, if the finished product is too brittle, it is possible to slightly rehydrate it.

1. Place the leather sheet back on the tray in the dehydrator.
2. Add a wet paper or fabric towel to a separate dehydrator tray.
3. Place the tray containing the towel beneath the tray containing the fragile sheet.
4. Place the machine's cover on it and allow it to sit. Do not heat the room.
5. Check back in a few hours or even the next day. The leather will have absorbed a portion of the air's moisture.
6. If the finished product is too sticky, return the tray to the dehydrator and continue drying at 15-minute intervals until the center is no longer sticky.

Vegetable Leather

Vegetable leathers are simple to prepare and can be used as wraps when rolled with your preferred spreads. These leathers can be frozen in plastic bags or canning jars for six to twelve months. They can be ground into a powder or mixed into soups or casseroles.

Dry pureed, cooked vegetables at 135 to 140 degrees Fahrenheit on trays in a dehydrator. The procedure is identical to that of fruit leather, except the cooked method is always used.

1. Choose, wash, and cut the vegetables into small pieces.
2. Cook the vegetables in a pan or skillet until tender.
3. Remove any surplus liquid.
4. Add seasonings to taste.
5. The mixture is blended into a thick puree.
6. Prepare drying trays and spread vegetable puree to within an inch of the edge. Using a ladle, scoop and evenly distribute the puree on the tray. The thickness should not exceed 14 inch, or the drying time will be affected. Therefore, the outer edges of the tray should be thicker than the interior. Using a ladle, redistribute the puree as desired by stirring it.
7. Dry at 135 to 140 degrees Fahrenheit for eight to twelve hours, or until the leather is finished. After it has dried, it will be translucent and slightly tacky. It will peel away from the plastic wrap or dehydrator sheet with ease. It's best to remove it while warm.

Vegetable leather can be used several ways:

- A savory, portable snack

- Paste for spaghetti sauce or pizza
- Reconstituted in soups

Highly Concentrated Food

During dehydration, fruits and vegetables lose between 80 and 90 percent of their moisture. This causes the food to be highly concentrated, smaller, and lighter, so the serving sizes can be deceptive. A cup of dehydrated apple chunks may not seem like much, but it required two to three medium-sized apples to produce. Would you really consume that many apples at once? How about tomatoes? One cup of diced tomatoes requires nine medium-sized tomatoes.

If you limit the amount of sugar in your diet, a significant portion of dried fruit will contain high levels of fructose, which may cause tooth decay in children.

Lastly, dehydrated foods contain more fiber. While fiber is beneficial in small doses, the high levels found in dried fruit can quickly cause intestinal issues such as gas, bloating, cramping, and diarrhea. It is best to be aware of portion sizes and extra calories so that you can adjust the size of your snacks accordingly.

CHAPTER 7: HOW TO MAKE JERKY

Once you have mastered the art of making jerky, you will be able to enhance your food storage plan. In addition to producing fruit and vegetables, you are now also producing an all-natural protein that is free of additives, food colorings, and preservatives.

You can make homemade jerky from any lean meat. Choose beef round, flank, chuck, rump, and brisket. The majority of pork, deer, turkey, and chicken cuts work well. Avoid highly marbled and fatty cuts of meat.

Safe Jerky

During the processing of jerky, the temperature of raw meat is of particular concern. You must use a dehydrator that reaches 160 degrees Fahrenheit in order to kill any harmful microorganisms on meat. If your dehydrator lacks a blowing fan and the ability to reach 160 degrees Fahrenheit, it cannot be used to make homemade jerky.

At all times, safe meat handling procedures must be observed. Use soap and water to wash your hands and clean utensils. Using the same cutting board, knife, or tongs on different batches of meat is never permissible.

Never allow frozen meat to thaw on the counter top. Bacteria (such as Staphylococcus aureus, Salmonella enteritidis, Escherichia coli O157:H7, and Campylobacter) can grow to dangerous levels and cause illness if food is left at room temperature for too long. Within the temperature range of 40 to 140 degrees Fahrenheit, bacteria double in number within 20 minutes. This temperature range is often referred to as the "Danger Zone." 8

Prepare the Meat

First, trim the meat of any visible fat and connective tissue. The flavor of rancid fat quickly becomes unpleasant. Using a fatty meat will drastically reduce the product's shelf life.

When meat is partially frozen, it is easier to cut, especially if you do not have an electric meat slicer. Cut it into 14-inch-thick strips between 1 and 112 inches wide and 4 to 8 inches long. The larger the meat cut, the longer it takes to dry. Cut with the grain of the meat for chewy jerky; slice against the grain for brittle jerky.

Pretreating the Meat

To prevent meat from spoiling, it is necessary to reduce the amount of bacteria on the meat. This can be accomplished by soaking the meat in vinegar, marinating and precooking the meat, or freezing the meat prior to cooking. If the meat has been frozen for sixty days, all bacteria have been destroyed, and neither soaking nor precooking is required.

Vinegar presoak. The meat should be sliced, placed in a large bowl, covered with a 5 percent vinegar solution, and allowed to soak for 10 minutes. Prepare the meat for marinating by removing it from the vinegar pre-soak and placing it in a plastic bag with a zip-top closure.

Add any brine ingredients to the bag of meat, ensuring that each piece of meat is completely covered.

If additional water is required, add it. Refrigerate overnight or for one to four hours. Drain before dehydrating.

Marinate and cook ahead. Cube the meat. Add the ingredients for the brine to the bag containing the meat, making sure that each piece of meat is completely covered. If additional water is required, add it. Refrigerate overnight or for one to four hours.

Precook the meat to decrease the likelihood of food-borne illness. Add the meat strips and marinade to a large pot and boil, uncovered, for five minutes, or until the internal temperature of the meat reaches 160°F. Drain.

Dehydrating the Jerky

Place the strips in a single layer on dehydrator sheets, pat each piece dry with a paper towel so that it is not dripping marinade, and ensure that they do not overlap or touch. It is not necessary to rinse. Dehydrate at 160°F. After four hours, examine the mixture and remove any dry, small pieces. Depending on the size of the slices, the entire process will take between four and six hours. Remove the dried strips from the trays and allow them to cool. When a piece of jerky can be bent, it is complete. It should crack and separate into strands, but not shatter.

If the meat strips were not marinated prior to dehydration, you may need to perform an additional drying step in the oven. Place the dried strips on a baking sheet and bake at 275°F for 10 minutes, or until the internal temperature of the jerky reaches 160°F. Before packaging for storage, eliminate any visible fat beads.

Creating Specialty Jerky Brines

There are numerous recipes for making jerky online. Ultimately, brine with flavor sets the stage for success. Once you have mastered the fundamentals of making brine, you are free to experiment and create a dish that your family will adore. Your specialty jerky brine must contain at least three of the following ingredients: salt, acid, sugar, and spice. Even savory marinades benefit from a touch of sweetness, so the majority of brine contains all four components.

Salt aids in preservation and imparts flavor. Try kosher salt, canning salt, sea salt, and table salt. Soy sauce is an alternative, but you should still add salt to your dish.

Wine, apple cider vinegar, balsamic vinegar, lemon juice, lime juice, soy sauce, white vinegar, and soy sauce are examples of acids.

Sugar, brown sugar, corn syrup, fruit juice, honey, and molasses are optional sweeteners.

Spices and seasonings are optional, but strongly recommended, and include dill seed, garlic, mustard seed, onion, paprika, pepper, red pepper, and virtually anything else.

Try out some of these combinations, peruse commercially prepared foods for inspiration, and prepare some of our favorite recipes from this book.

- Classic Beef
- Beef Steak
- Spicy Cajun
- Teriyaki
- Chile Lime

- Garlic Chili
- Hatch Chili and Onion
- Orange Chipotle
- Pineapple Orange

Storing Jerky

Jerky is not suitable for long-term storage. It can be stored for up to two weeks in sealed bags at room temperature. For the longest shelf life and flavor, homemade jerky can be refrigerated for up to one month or frozen for up to six months in airtight containers.

Rehydrating Jerky in Meals

The meat can be rehydrated and utilized effectively in soup and stew. In a large saucepan, combine 3 cups of water, 1 cup of beef jerky chunks, and any desired dehydrated vegetables. They must be completely submerged in water. Vegetables such as tomato, potato, bell pepper, onion, carrot, or garlic are recommended. If necessary, add additional water as the meat and vegetables expand. Permit the mixture to rest for thirty minutes to rehydrate. Place the pan over medium heat and bring the rehydrated ingredients to a boil. Add any fresh ingredients and spices, and simmer for an additional half-hour to one hour, until the jerky is tender and the fresh vegetables are cooked.

CHAPTER 8: SOUPS, POWDERS, AND HERBS

You may frequently find yourself with excess fruit, vegetables, and herbs that can be utilized. This chapter will discuss the advantages and disadvantages of dehydrating soup, as well as how to make your own specialized powders and dry herbs for tea and crafts.

Soups

Similar to making fruit and vegetable leather, soup can be made into a quick precooked meal that requires only hot water to revive. In contrast to leather, soup is first cooked on the stove and then dehydrated until crisp. Vegetables must be cooked for this to qualify as a quick meal. Otherwise, vegetables that have only been blanched during processing will remain partially uncooked. This method is most effective with thick soups, such as split pea, carrot, or winter squash, as they will remain on the trays rather than run off. A soup with a broth base is not recommended.

IS IT WORTH IT?

That depends on the types of meals you intend to cook. I tend to be the type of cook who takes a number of dry ingredients from the pantry, drops them into a pot of bouillon, broth, or water, and then prepares a delicious meal using the ingredients on hand. This method assumes you have the time to prepare homemade meals at home. If you need a homemade soup meal for busy days, travel, or backpacking trips, a soup that can be prepared in advance may be ideal. With one day of hard work and some planning, you can make a large batch of healthy soup that is simple to prepare, dehydrate, and store. Keep individual servings in jars in a cool, dark pantry for up to six months.

TIPS FOR SUCCESS

1. This method should only be applied to soups that are vegetarian, dairy-free, and low in fat. These ingredients will reduce the dry soup's shelf life. Do not select a recipe that calls for milk as the main ingredient unless you are willing to cook with water and add dry milk powder when packaging.
2. Cook the soup's ingredients on the stovetop until the desired consistency is reached. Keep in mind that the boiling water used for serving will not cook the food, only rehydrate it, so everything must be cooked thoroughly.
3. Consider using an immersion blender to chop the vegetables into uniformly smaller pieces prior to drying.
4. Typically, one serving of soup equals one dehydrator tray. Spread one or two ladles of soup on Paraflexx or plastic tray covers no thicker than 14 inch for rapid drying.
5. Dry on dehydrator trays for four to eight hours, or until soup has become brittle. It may be necessary to remove the soup from the tray and flip it halfway through the drying process.

6. Blend one tray of dry soup until it reaches a powdery consistency, and then measure it. This will help you determine how much is needed per serving.
7. Determine the amount of boiling water required to reconstitute one tray of soup to the desired consistency. Generally, 1 to 1½ cups of water is sufficient.
8. Package the soup in single-serving portions in canning jars. Ensure that there is enough room in the jars for the boiling water. These jars can withstand high temperatures without breaking or melting.
9. Create a recipe card with the name of the soup and serving instructions. Place it inside of each jar, listing the amount of water needed and any other ingredients that will complete the recipe.

Powders

Pulverized fruit powder can be purchased commercially, but it can be difficult to locate and expensive, particularly for home cooks. However, powdering your own fruits, vegetables, and spices is a cost-effective way to increase the nutritional value of your food storage on a budget.

Follow the dehydrating instructions in Chapter 9 for your favorite fruit or vegetable to get started. Food should be dried until it is devoid of moisture, so that when two pieces of produce are squeezed together, they do not adhere. To achieve the desired texture, fruits and vegetables should be dried in small pieces. Aim for the smoothness of copy paper. If the produce still feels moist, continue drying at two-hour intervals until it is completely dry.

A week of conditioning is required to remove any residual moisture from the dried product. Place the dried fruit in a plastic bag or canning jar, filling it no more than three-quarters of the way. Allow the fruit to sit, or condition, for two days, and shake the bag or jar once per day.

Due to their high sugar content, raisins, figs, plums, and apricots are naturally sticky when dehydrated. These should be dried into very small pieces if they are to be ground into powder. Even when using a well-dried fruit batch, stickiness is an inherent property of fruit powder. Add half to one teaspoon of arrowroot powder to the fruit before blending if the final product clumps; this will help to even out the clumps.

Using a food processor, blender, or coffee grinder, you can powder fruits and vegetables in small quantities. This is a tedious process that may require multiple attempts, but it is worthwhile.

The powder can be stored at room temperature for three months or in the refrigerator for six months. Be aware that homemade fruit and vegetable powder is not suitable for long-term storage, so only process as much powder as you anticipate needing within the next few months and leave the dried produce whole until you need another batch.

Here are some tasty ways to use homemade fruit or vegetable powder in your daily meals:

- Add it to meringue as a flavor enhancer and coloring agent
- Add fruit powder to your fermented beverages for a zingy second ferment
- Use it as a spice rub for meats
- Use it in glazes and frosting
- Add it to hot or cold cereal

- Add it to the batter of doughs for muffins, cakes, or quick bread. In any recipe, replace ½ cup flour with ½ cup fruit powder
- Add powder to smoothies. Make a fruit smoothie milkshake by adding ¼ cup fruit powder, 1 cup milk, 1 tablespoon honey, and ice cubes to a blender
- Use it when making homemade ice cream, frozen yogurt, or sorbet
- Rehydrate it for a fruit puree, like applesauce, at a later date

See the Tomato Powder recipe for a more detailed example.

Herbs

Herbs have been dried and used for home health and hearth for millennia; they constitute a significant portion of any emergency garden. You probably already have rosemary, chives, oregano, and mint on hand, to name a few.

Herbs that have been dried can be used to make herbal tea blends for protection against seasonal colds and flu, as well as to create your own rubs and spice blends for cooking. They have many independent applications:

- potpourri
- seasonings
- shampoo
- soap
- candles
- cleaners
- flavored vinegar
- herb-flavored oils
- tea blends

As time permits, you can dry herbs in small batches throughout the growing season. In the long run, purchasing individual plants and dehydrating them oneself is less expensive than purchasing dried herbs from a store. Your plants will thicken in response to regular pruning. Pruning keeps plants dense and prevents them from flowering and setting seed, allowing for multiple harvests.

Find aromatic herbs with large leaves. These 10 herbs are easy to cultivate and can be used for cooking, tea, and medicinal purposes.

- lemon verbena
- mint
- plantain
- rosemary
- basil
- bee balm
- chamomile

- ginger
- lemon balm
- stevia

Few regulations govern the harvesting and drying of herbs.

1. Collect flowers at the peak of their freshness. New leaves at the tips will have the highest flavor concentration.
2. On a sunny day, collect flowers and leaves just before the flowers open. The leaves must be completely dry, so harvest on a dry, sunny day in the middle of the morning, after the dew has evaporated, or in the early evening, before the dew forms.
3. Utilize scissors to harvest your crop. Leave four to six inches of stem on the plant for future development.
4. Once harvested, keep the herbs out of direct sunlight until the drying process can begin. Consider bringing along a basket and a towel to cover the cuttings as you harvest.

DRYING HERBS

As soon as possible, before they begin to wilt, commence drying freshly cut herbs. Remove any leaves or stems that are damaged or imperfect. Examine the crop for seeds and insects. Place these items in the compost pile.

To preserve the volatile oils in your herbs, you should minimize rinsing and handling as much as possible. Rinse the stems with cool water, gently shake off excess water, and pat dry with a towel. If you have a salad spinner, separate the leaves from the stems before spinning them. Using a large muslin towel as a spinner is an additional straightforward method for removing excess water. Simply place the wet leaves within the large towel, gather the corners, and swing it outside several times. The water will exit the towel as you spin it.

The purpose of this spinning is to get the leaves as dry as possible before beginning the dehydration process, so as to drastically reduce drying time. If you are cultivating organic herbs, you do not need to wash them unless they are extremely muddy or dirty.

Microwave drying. This method is only appropriate for herbs and is the quickest way to dry a small daily harvest. It is prepared in small batches of 1 or 2 cups. Spread one cup of clean leaves in a single layer between two sheets of paper towel and microwave in 30-second increments. If your oven has a wattage of 1,000 or more, you must take extra precautions to prevent leaves and paper from catching fire. Believe me; I know from experience!

Check the leaves after 30 seconds, then flip them over and heat for another 30 seconds. Remove small leaves as they finish drying, and repeat the process in 30-second intervals until the herbs are brittle. This will only require two or three minutes of your time.

Hanging. Although drying herbs by hanging them in the kitchen can add a homey touch, it is not the most efficient method. They will lose their flavor if left exposed to air and sunlight for an extended period of time.

To prevent this, cut stems should be laid out and sorted by size. Six to ten stalks should be bundled together and secured with a rubber band or twist tie. As the herbs dry, the rubber band will not become unfastened. The bundles should be hung away from direct sunlight and in a dry, well-ventilated space without excessive humidity. The bathroom is not an ideal location for this.

If you must dry them in direct sunlight, you should do so on a day with low humidity. Place the herb bundles in a paper bag with several ventilation holes. Attach the bag with clothespins to a string or clothesline. These bags must be brought inside at night to protect them from dew. The drying time will range from one to three days, based on the relative humidity in your home.

Display drying. The objective of screen drying is to allow air to circulate around the entire screen. Keep the screens elevated by placing blocks beneath them. Screens that are drying should not be placed in direct sunlight.

Because the herbs will shrink as they dry, they can touch each other on the screens. Screen drying is the slowest of the three methods. Due to the lack of airflow, drying will take between two and four days.

Dehydrator drying. Using a dehydrator to dry herbs can be quite simple. Separate the leaves from the stems and arrange them in a single layer no more than 14 inch thick. It's okay for them to touch; dried herbs will not stick together.

Herbs are dried at a lower temperature than fruits and vegetables in order to prevent the essential oils from evaporating during the drying process. For optimal results, dry between 90 and 100 degrees Fahrenheit. Herbs with strong flavors, such as garlic, ginger, and rosemary, should be dried separately from herbs with milder flavors, which may absorb their flavors. From two hours for leafy herbs to six hours for woody stems or roots, drying times vary.

STORING HERBS

Once your herbs have been dried to the point where they can be easily powdered between your fingers, they are ready for storage. If you haven't already, remove the leaves from the stalks and keep the leaves intact. Do not crush the leaves until you are ready to use them in your teas, tonics, and lotions, as this will release the aromatic oils you desire. To use the herbs, crush the leaves with your hands, a mortar and pestle, or a rolling pin, and then measure according to the recipe's instructions. Use dried herbs sparingly; you'll need about one-third as much as you would fresh herbs in your recipes.

Keep the leaves in containers that are airtight. Mason jars work well, but any repurposed glass container with a lid will suffice. Glass is ideal because metal and plastic can alter the flavor of certain herbs, and the flavor will eventually transfer to the container. I stored peppermint in a gallon-sized plastic jug. It has been there for several years. The herbs are still fragrant, but I will never be able to store anything else in the jar again; the aroma has permeated the container entirely. It is peppermint or nothing from now on!

One year is the recommended storage period for herbs. It is best practice to cultivate enough fresh herbs to last between harvests. After one year, the herbs will still be edible, but their aroma will diminish. I use my aging herbs to make soaps and crafts. Herbs should always be stored in a cool, dark location away from heat. If you have a large harvest of your favorite herb, you can remove the oxygen from the jar and freeze the herbs in FoodSaver containers. As long as you keep moisture out of the container, you can store food in the freezer for up to 18 months.

CHAPTER 9: DEHYDRATING 50 COMMON FRUIT AND VEGETABLES

This chapter will demystify the dehydration of your favorite fruits and vegetables. You may even discover foods that you were unaware could be dehydrated for home storage. Each entry details the optimal methods for cleaning, chopping, drying, and rehydrating individual pantry items for future use.

Apples

Apples are first on the list and may be the fruit with which dehydration is easiest to commence. After they have been cleaned, minimal preparation is required. We prefer to keep the apple skin on for the fiber and nutrients it provides. They independently prepare a nutritious snack.

Refer to page 28 for cleaning instructions on apples that are not organic. Wash all organic fruits and vegetables with warm water. Cloths are utilized to dry apples.

Use an apple peeler/corer to create slices of uniform thickness. Alternately, core and cut the apple into eight equal-sized pieces, or use a mandoline.

Recommended thickness: 1/8 inch for chips and a small dice for baking.

Drying time: 6 to 12 hours, depending on thickness

Temperature: 125°F

Consistency when dry: Leathery to crisp, with no moisture in the middle

Blanching requirements: N/A

Oxidizing treatment: Treat cut pieces with ascorbic acid or lemon juice.

How to rehydrate: Pour boiling water over the dried apples until just covered and let pieces soak for 30 minutes, or until they rehydrate to the consistency you are looking for.

Consistency when rehydrated: Like cooked apples (soft)

Yield: 2 to 3 medium apples = 1 cup dried apples = 1¼ cups rehydrated apples

Apricots

Apricots are well worth the wait, despite their lengthy drying period. Rehydrate for use in pies and other desserts; use dried as a healthy snack.

For non-organic apricots, cleaning instructions can be found on page 28. Wash and dry organic apricots with warm water.

To prepare, remove the pit. No skins need to be removed.

Cut the material in half or quarters for a quicker drying time.

Eight to twelve hours for quarters; twelve to twenty-four hours for halves.

Temperature: 125°F

Texture when dry: Leathery

Non-existent requirements for blanching

To preserve their light color, use lemon juice or ascorbic acid as an oxidizing agent.

How to replenish fluids: Soak for 15 to 20 minutes in hot water or warmed juice, or simmer on the stovetop, until the fruit is plump and has absorbed the liquid.

When rehydrated, the consistency is soft and plump.

2 pounds of fresh apricots equals 6 ounces of dried apricots, which yields 2 cups of rehydrated apricots.

Asparagus

Our household enjoys asparagus so much that we could eat it every day for weeks. The growing season is brief, and asparagus is expensive when it is out of season. To keep our favorite vegetable on the table and save money, we dehydrate it as much as possible. Powderize the dried ingredients and add them to soup.

Follow the cleaning directions on page 28 for non-organic asparagus. Wash organic asparagus with warm water and pat dry thoroughly.

To prepare, remove the tough ends first.

Pieces with a thickness of 1 inch are suggested.

Drying time: eight to twelve hours

Temperature: 125°F

Durability when dry: Brittle

Requirements for blanching: three to four minutes

Oxidizing treatment: N/A

How to replenish fluids: Soak 1 cup of asparagus in 214 cups of boiling water for 30 minutes, or directly add dried pieces to soup.

Consistency when rehydrated: Similar to cooked texture

2 cups of fresh asparagus equals 1 cup of dried asparagus equals 112 cups of rehydrated asparagus.

Bananas

Without the use of unnecessary additives, it is nearly impossible for a home food processor to replicate the texture of store-bought banana chips. Did you know that bananas are dipped in sugar syrup and then deep-fried in order to achieve their extra sweetness and crispness? As you're dehydrating fresh bananas for your food storage, I'm assuming you're trying to avoid unnecessary additives and calories.

Use rehydrated banana in smoothies and cereals, or serve the pieces on their own after chilling. Or simply consume as chips!

Clean: Wash and dry before peeling. There is no distinction between organic and nonorganic products.

How to get ready: The bananas with the best flavor are slightly green on top and have brown spots on the peel. Use ripe bananas to create leather.

Recommended chip thickness: 1/8-inch rounds

Drying time: eight to twelve hours

Temperature: 125°F

Dry consistency: Brittle and easily broken

Non-existent requirements for blanching

To prevent browning, use lemon juice as a dipping or spraying solution.

How to replenish fluids: Mix one part water with one part chips, then simmer for five minutes at a low temperature.

Consistency following rehydration: Like fresh

5 large bananas yield 2 cups of dried bananas, which rehydrate to yield 4 cups of bananas.

Beans (Green, Yellow, Snap)

The green bean is a healthy, pantry-stable vegetable that is simple to dehydrate and good for you. While we enjoy eating fresh beans from the garden, I prefer to purchase frozen beans in bulk from the supermarket for dehydrating. This is due to the fact that I dislike the cutting and blanching required for fresh beans. Thankfully, the local grocery store carries a wide variety of organic beans, so my processing time has been drastically reduced. The peak season for green beans is from April to October, and one pound will yield approximately three cups of beans.

For non-organic beans, follow the cleaning instructions on page 28. Wash organic beans in warm water and pat them dry.

How to get ready: Remove any unnecessary strings. Before blanching, cut vegetables. There is no preparation required when dehydrating from a frozen state.

Suggested thickness: 112-inch pieces or 4-inch-long thin strips cut lengthwise.

Drying time: eight to fourteen hours

Temperature: 125°F

Dry consistency: hard and brittle

Requirements for blanching: Boil or steam blanch for two to three minutes.

Oxidizing treatment: N/A

How to replenish fluids: Soak 1 cup of green beans in 214 cups of warm water for 30 minutes, or until plump. Or, add to soup directly without rehydrating.

Consistency following rehydration: Like fresh

2 cups fresh beans equal 1 cup dried beans, which yields 2 cups rehydrated beans.

Beets

Late in the autumn, before the ground freezes, harvest beets for storage. They have the best flavor when their diameter is 2 inches. Except for gold varieties, when cut, beets "bleed" their color.

Scrub both organic and conventional beets with a vegetable brush and warm water.

How to get ready: In a large saucepan, cover with water and cook until tender, about 45 minutes. Place the pot under cold running water and rinse the beets until they are manageable.

Peel and then slice into 1/8-inch strips, as suggested.

Drying time: eight to twelve hours; stir every four hours.

Temperature: 125°F

Hard consistency when dry

Non-existent requirements for blanching

No oxidizing treatment

How to rehydrate: Soak 1 cup of dry beets for 1.5 hours in 234 cups of warm water.

Consistency after rehydration: Similar to cooked

2 cups fresh beets yield 1 cup dried beets, which yields 112 cups rehydrated beets.

Blueberries

If you are fortunate enough to be able to grow blueberries at home, you are in for a treat. If properly stored in a cool, dry location of your pantry, dehydrated blueberries will last for more than a year. Use frozen berries to bypass the preparation time.

As with the processing of cranberries (page 25), the blueberry's outer shell must be pierced to ensure that the heat reaches the interior and dries the berry completely. This can be done by piercing each berry individually, which is time-consuming, or by placing them in a metal strainer and submerging them in boiling water for 30 seconds. It is not necessary to perform the additional water bath processing or piercing when using frozen berries.

Add rehydrated blueberries to muffins and pancakes, or make Blueberry Basil Syrup using the recipe on page 83.

For non-organic blueberries, please refer to page 28 for cleaning instructions. Rinse delicately. Rinse organic berries with warm water, then pat them dry with care.

How to get ready: Remove stems. Each berry should be pierced with a skewer or pin, blanched for thirty seconds, or frozen until solid.

Suggestion for thickness: Leave intact

Time to dry: 10 to 18 hours

Temperature: 125 to 135 degrees Fahrenheit

Dry consistency: rigid, does not stick together when squeezed.

Requirements for blanching: See notes above.

No oxidizing treatment

How to replenish fluids: Ten to fifteen minutes of submersion in cool water.

Rehydrated consistency: not as plump or juicy as fresh. Use without rehydrating in baked goods to keep the moisture content low.

2 pints of fresh blueberries are equivalent to 1 cup of dried blueberries and 2 cups of rehydrated blueberries.

Broccoli

Broccoli is an excellent food to keep on hand. I enjoy grinding broccoli stalks for use in broccoli soup. Rehydrating dried florets for soup, stew, or even a side dish is possible. Look for a head with closed flowers and a deep color.

Clean: For non-organic broccoli, refer to page 28 for cleaning instructions. Wash and pat dry organic broccoli with warm water.

How to get ready: Separate the head from the stem. Separate the florets into pieces of equal size. Cut the stalk into pieces of equal size.

Recommended thickness: pieces of equal size

Time required to dry: 8 to 12 hours; stalks may require longer.

Temperature: 125°F

Durability when dry: Crisp

Blanching requirements: For florets, blanch in boiling water for two minutes or in steam for three minutes. Cook the stalks for five minutes in boiling water until tender, then drain.

No oxidizing treatment

How to replenish fluids: Soak 1 cup of cauliflower in 2 cups of water. Soak for 30 to 60 minutes, or until no longer absorbent. There is no need to soak broccoli if it will be added to a recipe that contains water and requires cooking.

Consistency following rehydration: Fresh-tasting, but not crunchy

2 cups of fresh broccoli is equivalent to 1 cup of dried broccoli and 2 cups of rehydrated broccoli.

Cabbage and Brussels Sprouts

Even if cabbage is not the first vegetable on your dehydrating list, it should be among the top 10. Due to its nutritional benefits, it is recommended for your pantry. Cabbage is at its peak between October and January, and one pound of cabbage yields six cups of freshly shred leaves. When fresh, a tightly wrapped head of lettuce will last 14 days in the refrigerator. However, if you take the time to dehydrate the lettuce, the leaves will remain "as fresh" for an entire year. This method works for all types of cabbage, and it is even odorless as it dries! Check out the recipe for Slow Cooker Stuffed Cabbage Rolls on page 115 to use your dried cabbage.

Clean: For cleaning non-organic cabbage, follow the instructions on page 28. Wash and pat dry organic cabbage with cool water.

How to get ready: Remove the outer leaves and stem, and then remove the core from the head. Thinly slice into strips.

Recommended thickness: 1/8-inch shreds or entire leaves

Drying time: eight to twelve hours

Temperature: 125°F

Dry consistency: pliable and dry, like paper

Non-existent requirements for blanching

No oxidizing treatment

How to replenish fluids: Soak one part of dried cabbage in three parts of cool water for three minutes, or directly add pieces to soup.

Consistency following rehydration: similar to fresh but not as crisp

3 cups fresh cabbage equals 1 cup dried cabbage, which rehydrates to 3 cups fresh cabbage.

Carrots

Carrots are a pantry staple for me. We use them frequently in stir-fry dishes and soups. They lose more than 80 percent of their water during dehydration and will shrink to almost nothing when they are completely dry. Consider this and use tray inserts when drying them, or you may discover that they have fallen through to the dehydrator's bottom.

Clean: Follow the cleaning instructions on page 28 and scrub non-organic carrots with a vegetable brush. Scrub carrots grown organically with a vegetable brush and warm water in a colander. No need to peel.

How to get ready: Trim the top and bottom by 1/8 inch, then cut into rounds or cubes.

Thinness suggestions: 18-inch rounds; 14-inch cubes; shredded

Drying time: ten to twelve hours

Temperature: 125°F

Dry consistency: hard and brittle

Blanch vegetables in boiling water for three to four minutes, or until they are bright orange.

No oxidizing treatment

How to replenish fluids: To achieve a raw-like texture, soak for 15 to 30 minutes in cool water. To prepare cooked carrots, combine carrots and water in a 1:1 ratio, bring to a boil, cover, and cook over low heat for 10 minutes. Add to soup or stew without rehydrating first.

Consistency when rehydrated: Anywhere from crunchy to just-cooked, depending on rehydrating method

Yield: 2 cups fresh carrots = 1 cup dried carrots = 1¼ cups rehydrated carrots

Cauliflower

Cauliflower can be utilized in numerous ways besides as a side dish. It is pureed and used as a thickening agent in soup and stew. If you grate it into small pieces (ricing), you can rehydrate it and use it as a substitute for pizza crust or mashed potatoes. Try Cauliflower Soup (page 111) or Cauliflower Rice Pizza Crust (page 111). (page 120).

The peak season for cauliflower is September to November, and a typical head weighs two pounds. Each pound of fresh cauliflower will lose 75 percent of its water and become a quarter pound when dried, so dehydration is a great way to preserve this nutritious vegetable.

Clean: Cauliflower, both organic and nonorganic, is washed and dried with warm water. If the broccoli is freshly harvested from the garden, soak it in salt water for 10 minutes to kill any insects.

How to get ready: Remove large stalks and outer leaves from the plant.

Recommended thickness: Cut the cauliflower into small, uniform 1- to 2-inch florets or rice it and place it on fruit leather trays to dry.

Drying time: eight to twelve hours

Temperature: 125°F

Durability when dry: Crisp

Blanching requirements: Steam the florets for four to five minutes to keep them white. If you will be using it as an ingredient and the color is irrelevant, you can skip this step. Cook large stalks until tender, then slice and place on trays.

No oxidizing treatment

How to replenish fluids: Soak 1 cup of cauliflower for 15 to 20 minutes in 1 cup of water.

Consistency following rehydration: Like cooked

4 cups fresh cauliflower yields 1 cup dried cauliflower which rehydrates to 4 cups fresh cauliflower.

Celery

Although celery is such a versatile vegetable, most individuals rarely consume the entire stalk before it spoils. We dehydrate ours to ensure a constant supply for soup and stew. Don't forget to grind it and create celery salt for savory salads and spice blends.

One celery head is sufficient to fill two trays in my Nesco Gardenmaster dehydrator. Consider including a catch tray to prevent the smaller pieces from slipping through after they have dried.

Clean: For non-organic celery, refer to page 28 for cleaning instructions. Wash organic celery in warm water, then pat dry.

How to get ready: Separate the stalks and trim the ends. If you are making celery powder, you should retain the leaves.

Leaves and smaller celery pieces should be placed on a separate tray from the larger stalks. These will dry in half the time, and there will be no need to separate them from the rest of the batch.

Recommended thickness: half-inch chunks

Four hours for leaves and eight to twelve hours for stalk fragments to dry

Temperature: 125°F

Texture when dry: Crisp

Requirements for blanching: Steam for one minute if you intend to rehydrate in whole pieces. If you intend to make powder, omit.

No oxidizing treatment

How to replenish fluids: Place whole pieces in warm water for 10 to 15 minutes, or add to soup or stew directly.

Consistency following rehydration: Soft, like cooked

3 cups of fresh celery equals 1 cup of dried celery equals 2 cups of rehydrated celery

Cherries

Some individuals prefer to blanch their cherries for 30 seconds in boiling water before dehydrating them. It is an unnecessary step that does not enhance the quality of the dried fruit, in my opinion. To preserve the color of dried cherries of a lighter variety, such as Rainier or Emperor Francis, an oxidizing treatment may be necessary.

For non-organic cherries, please follow the cleaning instructions on page 28. Warm water is used to clean organic cherries, which are then dried.

How to get ready: Remove the stem, cut the fruit in half, and remove the pit.

Utilize a skewer and water bottles as a pitter for cherries.

Whole or half is suggested thickness

Drying time: 12 to 24 hours Temperature: 125 degrees Fahrenheit

Dry consistency: The dried cherries should not stick together and should make a crackling sound when dropped on a countertop.

Specifications for bleaching: Your preference

Treatment by oxidation: Your preference

How to replenish fluids: Simmer on the stovetop until the food is rehydrated. Use in baked goods and syrup.

Consistency following rehydration: Chewy

10 ounces of fresh cherries are equivalent to 1 cup of dried cherries, or 1 1/2 cups rehydrated.

Citrus

Purchase citrus with thin skins for the best flavor and juice. The peels can be utilized whole or as a powder in a variety of recipes. Dried pieces can be steeped in vinegar to aid in cleaning, added to water to make a tasty drink, or candied. The pith may be utilized to produce natural pectin. Mix the powdered peels with sugar, make lemon pepper spice, or incorporate them into scones and baked goods. Substitute for extract or zest.

Before dehydration, all store-bought citrus must be washed to remove the wax coating.

Follow the guidelines on page 28 for cleaning non-organic citrus fruits. Wash and dry organic fruits with warm water.

How to get ready: Utilize a mandoline for uniform cuts. Save the ends for use in a vinegar-based cleaner by allowing them to dry. Remove the pith and then cut the fruit into strips.

Recommended thickness: 1/8-inch slices

Drying time: between four and eight hours

Temperature: 125°F

Texture when dry: Crisp

Non-existent requirements for blanching

No oxidizing treatment

How to replenish fluids: For 10 to 15 minutes, cover with cool water.

Consistency following rehydration: Like fresh

1 medium orange or 2 to 3 lemons yield one cup of dehydrated citrus rounds, one tablespoon of citrus powder, and three-quarters of a cup of rehydrated citrus rounds.

With the rest of the batch, dry the citrus ends and save them to make cleaning vinegar infused with citrus. To use, add dried citrus ends and white vinegar to a canning jar. Give the mixture one to two weeks to steep. Strain the citrus peels and dispose of them in the compost. The vinegar can be diluted 1:1 with water while retaining its fresh aroma.

Coconut

If coconut is available in the supermarket, you should experiment with drying it yourself. The fresh flavor of homemade dried coconut is well worth the trouble. Additionally, it produces nutritious milk for drinking and flour for baking. See Shredded Coconut (page 96), Coconut Flour (page 97), and Sweet Potato Coconut Flour Pancakes for ways to use dehydrated coconut (page 114).

Clean: Wash and dry, then follow the instructions listed below. There is no distinction between organic and nonorganic products.

How to get ready: Drill a hole in the nut's cap and drain the water. halved in half Remove the outer bark and skin before shredding or slicing the meat into pieces of equal size.

Shred or cut into 38-inch pieces is the suggested thickness.

Drying time: between four and eight hours

Temperature: 125°F

Dry consistency: leathery to crisp

Non-existent requirements for blanching

No oxidizing treatment

How to replenish fluids: Add double the amount of hot water to the coconut and soak for 30 minutes.

Consistency following rehydration: Like fresh

Yield: 1 small coconut = 1 cup dehydrated coconut = 1½ cups coconut flour = ¾ cup rehydrated coconut

Corn

Due to where we live, we consume a great deal of corn but do not grow it ourselves. Central Texas is corn country, and the field next door is filled with acres and acres of GMO corn. Corn is a wind-pollinated crop, so it is likely that cross-pollination would occur between the GMO corn and the open-pollinated crops I would be growing. Instead, I buy organic frozen corn in bulk from Costco. There is no need for cutting or blanching, which saves a great deal of time.

For non-organic corn, follow the cleaning instructions on page 28. Wash organic corn in warm water and pat it dry. There is no need to clean frozen corn.

How to get ready: Remove the tassels from each corn cob and shuck the ears. Cook whole ears of corn in boiling water for six to eight minutes, or until tender. Transfer the corn to a bowl containing ice water and allow it to cool. Utilize a decobber or a knife with a sharp blade to remove the kernels from the cob. Spread out the kernels on the dehydrator trays.

Individual kernels are suggested thickness

Six to eight hours for fresh; eight to ten hours for frozen.

Temperature: 125°F

Durability when dry: Brittle

Requirements for blanching: See above.

No oxidizing treatment

How to replenish fluids: Soak 1 cup of corn in 214 cups of water for 30 minutes. Or, add to soups, stews, and skillet dishes.

Consistency following rehydration: as freshly cooked

2 cups of fresh corn kernels equal 1 cup of dried corn kernels, yielding 112 cups of rehydrated corn.

Cucumbers

When we think of preserving cucumbers, we typically consider making pickles, but dehydrating them can add a new dimension to your soups and sauces. You can process dehydrated cucumber chips into a powder and add it to homemade salad dressing (see Creamy Cucumber Salad Dressing on page 90). Or, you can add them to your morning smoothies or spice up your zucchini chips using the recipe on page 106.

For cleaning non-organic cucumbers, please refer to page 28. Wash and dry organic cucumbers with warm water.

Prepare by slicing into rounds.

Recommended thickness: 14 inch

Four to six hours for drying

Temperature: 135°F

Dry consistency: brittle; should break when bent.

Non-existent requirements for blanching

No oxidizing treatment

Soak in cool water for 30 to 60 minutes to rehydrate.

Consistency when rehydrated: crisp flavor and a limp consistency

Yield: 1 cup fresh cucumber = ¼ cup dehydrated cucumber = ¾ cup rehydrated cucumber

Cucumber slices can be rehydrated with a pickle brine. (For the recipe for Dehydrated Refrigerator Pickles, see page 108.) They will be just as crunchy as homemade pickles from the refrigerator. Alternatively, you can dehydrate a jar of store-bought chips or pickle spears. Your family will enjoy the change in texture, and it's much easier to transport than a messy pickle. The finished pickle chips are extremely salty, and it is easy to consume the entire jar in one sitting.

Eggplant

Eggplant will darken if not blanched prior to processing and storage, despite its use in eggplant and tomato casseroles. Oriental eggplant is long and slender, and its flavor is milder than that of standard supermarket eggplant. It is an outstanding garden plant for USDA Plant Hardiness Zones 4 through 11.

Follow the cleaning instructions on page 28 for non-organic eggplant. Wash and pat dry organic eggplant with warm water.

Prepare by dicing, slicing, or cubing. Prepare as you would for cooking purposes.

Recommended thickness: 14 inch

Drying time: six to twelve hours

Temperature: 125°F

Texture when dry: Leathery

Requirements for blanching include 15 seconds in boiling water.

No oxidizing treatment

To rehydrate eggplant, combine equal parts eggplant and cool water, and then soak for 30 minutes.

When rehydrated, the texture is somewhat leathery, but the flavor resembles that of cooked eggplant.

2 cups of fresh eggplant equals 1 cup of dried eggplant, which rehydrates to 114 cups.

Figs

As they dry, figs become exceedingly sticky. Ensure that they do not overlap, or they will adhere. Consider lining the baking trays with parchment paper to facilitate cleanup. Ensure that only ripe fruit is utilized for this project. If your figs stick together, lightly toss them with sugar prior to storage.

For any recipe that calls for peaches, pears, prunes, or dates, figs can be substituted successfully. Prepare Oatmeal Fig Cookies on page 133 to sample these fruits.

For cleaning non-organic figs, please refer to page 28. Wash and pat dry organic figs with warm water.

To prepare fresh figs, remove the stems and cut away any imperfections. Perforate the skin if drying small figs whole.

Recommended thickness: halve or quarter. Place figs skin-side down on the tray.

Drying time is variable. Start checking at eight hours; completion could take up to 24 hours. Turning the fruit could accelerate the process.

Temperature: 125°F

Dry consistency: leathery and flexible

Requirements for blanching: If drying figs whole, immerse in boiling water for 30 seconds.

No oxidizing treatment

How to replenish fluids: Cover with boiling water, then let stand for 30 minutes.

Rehydrated consistency: Not typically rehydrated. Used as snacks and in cooking when dried.

2 cups of fresh figs yield 1 cup of dried figs

A few hours in the dehydrator will lengthen the shelf life of dried figs purchased from a store.

Garlic

We keep garlic seasoning in our pantry and use it with nearly every meal. After the first frost, garlic is planted in the fall, and there are over 50 varieties of soft-neck and hard-neck garlic adapted to every growing region. If possible, grow and preserve your own garlic; the fresh flavor will be worth the effort. TheGarlicStore.com, SeedSavers.org, and TerritorialSeed.com all sell garlic cloves suitable for planting. Using the square-foot gardening method, nine cloves can be grown per square foot.

If you are not the gardening type, you can save a great deal of time by purchasing large jars of organic garlic from a big box store. A 32-ounce container costs approximately $14 and yields about 8 ounces of garlic powder when dried.

Separate and peel organic and nonorganic garlic cloves, then cut off the root ends.

How to get ready: Utilize a mandoline or a food processor to cut the vegetables.

See above for proposed thickness.

Drying time: six to twelve hours

Temperature: 125°F

Texture when dry: Crisp

Non-existent requirements for blanching

No oxidizing treatment

How to replenish fluids: Use as a powder or shred for soup or stir-fry.

Consistency following rehydration: Like cooked

1 cup fresh garlic equals 1/4 cup dehydrated garlic, which rehydrates to yield 34 cup.

Store the dried garlic in an airtight container in the freezer, and then grind it as needed. It will remain fresh for more than a year if stored in this manner.

Ginger

Since candied ginger is costly, we make our own. The cooking process also produces ginger syrup, which can be bottled and used to flavor ginger ale, pancakes, or your preferred oatmeal. Refer to page 132 for our recipe for candied ginger!

Wash and dry both organic and nonorganic ginger with warm water.

How to get ready: If making candied ginger, peel.

Suggestion: 1/8-inch thick slices

Four to six hours for drying

Temperature: 135°F

Dry consistency: Flexible

No cooking is necessary when chopping ginger for ground use. For instructions on making candied ginger, see page 132.

No oxidizing treatment

Typically, rehydration is not necessary. Instead, chop the herb and incorporate it into salads, cookies, gingerbread, or herbal tea.

Nonexistent consistency when rehydrated

1 cup fresh ginger equals 1/2 cup dried ginger equals 3/4 cup rehydrated ginger

Grapes

If you have the good fortune to cultivate your own grapes, you have an advantage. The Environmental Working Group's (EWG) list of the "Dirty Dozen" consistently ranks commercially grown grapes in the top 10 for pesticide contamination. Pay close attention to cleaning your nonorganic grapes prior to dehydrating them.

For non-organic grapes, please follow the cleaning instructions on page 28. Warm water is used to clean organic grapes, which are then dried.

How to get ready: After blanching, remove from stems.

Suggestion for thickness: Leave intact

Drying time: 15 to 30 hours, size dependent

Temperature: 135°F

Dry consistency: Flexible

Exceptions to requirements: 30 seconds in boiling water followed by 30 seconds in ice water. This prepares the skins for further processing and halves the drying time.

No oxidizing treatment

How to rehydrate: Not Applicable

Rehydration consistency: dried grapes are raisins and cannot be reconstituted. Use dried in cooking or as a snack.

1 cup of fresh grapes equals 1/4 cup of raisins

Tea made from dried and powdered grape leaves is delicious. Wash and pat the leaves dry. Three hours later, stir the grapes that have been piled on dehydrator trays no thicker than half an inch. Approximately six hours at 90 degrees Fahrenheit, or until crisp.

Green Onions and Leeks

Onions and leeks dehydrate remarkably well and with little effort. Look for them to go on sale between August and December, their peak season, and stock up.

Clean: Wash both organic and conventional onions with cool water and pat dry.

How to get ready: Remove the root ends, trim the tops by 14 inch, and remove any limp leaves.

Recommended thickness: Cut into half-inch thick rings.

Drying time: eight to twelve hours

Temperature: 125°F

Papery consistency when dry

Non-existent requirements for blanching

No oxidizing treatment

Add directly to soup or spritz with cool water to rehydrate.

Consistency following rehydration: Like fresh

2 cups of fresh green onions equal 1 cup of dried green onions, which rehydrates to 114 cups.

Separate white ends from green stalks on dehydrator trays. The tops will dry at different rates, preventing you from removing the dried portions while waiting for the remainder to finish.

Horseradish

The horseradish plant is making a comeback in modern gardens. Each fall, harvest the roots and leave enough for the following year's crop. Blend 1/4 cup grated root, 1 tablespoon mustard, 1 teaspoon vinegar, 1 cup sour cream, and salt and pepper to taste in a blender.

Clean: Wash both organic and conventional horseradish with warm water and a vegetable brush before drying.

How to get ready: Remove rootlets and stem fragments. Scrape and peel the root.

Recommendation for thickness: grate and spread evenly on dehydrator trays.

Drying time: between four and eight hours

Temperature: 125°F

Durability when dry: Brittle

Non-existent requirements for blanching

No oxidizing treatment

How to replenish fluids: Soak 1 cup of horseradish in 1 cup of warm water for 30 minutes;

rehydration is not required if horseradish is being used in cooking.

Consistency following rehydration: Like fresh

1 cup fresh horseradish equals 12 cup dehydrated horseradish, which rehydrates to 34 cup.

Until needed, store the horseradish pieces in a vacuum-sealed jar. Break off a portion and grind it in a coffee grinder reserved for pungent herbs and spices.

Kale

Currently, kale is popular as a health food. It is a rich source of iron, vitamin K, and vitamin A, as well as potent antioxidants. Dehydrate to make powder for smoothies (refer to page 46 for powdering instructions), or experiment with making your own seasoned Kale Chips (page 105).

Clean: For cleaning non-organic kale, please refer to page 28. Wash organic kale in cool water and pat dry.

How to get ready: Remove the stems by pinching or slicing them off.

Pieces with a thickness of 2 to 3 inches

Drying time: between two and six hours

Temperature: 135°F

Dry consistency: crisp and papery

Non-existent requirements for blanching

No oxidizing treatment

How to replenish fluids: Use in smoothies or soup, or consume as chips.

Consistency following rehydration: Like cooked

2 cups fresh kale equals 1 cup dried kale, which yields 2 cups rehydrated kale.

Kiwi

If the conditions are favorable, kiwi can grow prolifically on a vine in fairly acidic soil. It requires one male plant for every eight female plants, sturdy support, and at least 240 days without frost. The best uses for dried kiwi are as snacks and in fresh salads.

Clean: Wash and dry both organic and nonorganic kiwis with warm water.

How to get ready: Remove peel.

Thickness recommendation: 38- to 1/2-inch slices. If pieces come into contact with one another on the trays, they will adhere.

Drying time: six to twelve hours

Temperature: 125°F

Dry consistency: flexible and non-sticky

Non-existent requirements for blanching

Use a lemon juice dip as an oxidizing agent if you wish to preserve the vibrant color.

Spray until plump or eat dry as snacks to rehydrate.

Consistency following rehydration: Like fresh

2 cups of fresh kiwi yield 1 cup of dried kiwi and 1 1⁄2 cups of rehydrated kiwi.

Lettuce

During the growing season, we frequently have excess lettuce, and it seems wasteful to send it all to the compost bin. Some of the specialty spring mixes can become quite bitter when dried; therefore, you should experiment to determine which type of lettuce meets your needs. Also, skip drying iceberg lettuce. It is not worth the dehydrator space required to dry it because it has little nutritional value. Typically, lettuce is not rehydrated.

Follow the cleaning guidelines on page 28 for non-organic lettuce. Wash and pat dry organic lettuce with cool water.

How to get ready: Separate the leaves from the stem and remove any thick stems or veins, as they will slow the drying process.

Recommended thickness: single or half leaves

Four to six hours for drying

Temperature: 110°F

Papery consistency when dry

Non-existent requirements for blanching

No oxidizing treatment

Use as a powder for smoothies or in a green powder blend to rehydrate.

Nonexistent consistency when rehydrated

1 cup of fresh lettuce yields 1⁄4 cup of dehydrated lettuce leaves, or roughly 1 tablespoon of lettuce leaf powder.

Mangoes or Papayas

These tasty treats have become a standard topping for morning yogurt. Mango and papaya can be rehydrated for use in smoothies and syrup.

Follow the instructions on page 28 to clean mangoes and papayas that are not organic. Wash organic produce with warm water and pat dry.

How to get ready: Using a vegetable peeler, remove the skin before slicing the flesh into large, flat sections from top to bottom. Because the fruit is slippery, a mandoline is an effective tool.

Thickness recommendation: 3/8-inch slices or wedges Utilize parchment paper to prevent adhesion. If pieces are sliced too thinly, they will stick to dehydrator trays.

Drying time: six to twelve hours

Temperature: 125°F

Dry consistency: flexible and papery, but not sticky

Non-existent requirements for blanching

Optional oxidizing treatment: Spray lemon juice over the trays as they are being filled.

How to replenish fluids: Cover with boiling water and let stand for 15 minutes.

Consistency following rehydration: Like fresh

2 cups of fresh mango equals 1 cup of dried mango equals 112 cups of rehydrated mango.

Melons

We can never produce enough watermelons to keep the children satisfied, so we purchase them during their peak season and dehydrate them. A few long slices of dry honeydew or cantaloupe make for an excellent afternoon snack.

Clean: The exterior of both organic and nonorganic melons should be washed with dish soap and warm water, then patted dry.

How to get ready: Remove the flesh from the rind and cut the melon into uniform cubes. For slices, halve the melon and remove the seeds. Cut the melon into eight sections, remove the rind, and then cut each section into five smaller pieces.

Recommended thickness: 14- to 1/2-inch slices, 112-inch dice

Time to dry: eight to ten hours

Temperature: 125°F

Dry consistency: Flexible, with dry centers

Non-existent requirements for blanching

No oxidizing treatment

How to replenish fluids: Typically consumed as dried snacks or as a garnish in oatmeal or yogurt.

Soft consistency when rehydrated

2 cups of fresh melon equals 1 cup of dried melon equals 112 cups of rehydrated melon

Mushrooms

Some chefs would never consider storing food without first washing it. Perhaps mushrooms are the exception. Mushrooms that are wet will turn black and not dry well. However, commercially grown mushrooms are grown in a soilless medium of sterilized hardwood sawdust or straw, making them safe to consume without washing. For those with a texture aversion to mushrooms, they can be dehydrated and ground into a powder.

The umami flavor released by mushrooms gives soups, stews, meatloaf, burger patties, and omelets depth.

Clean: Before processing, wash with cool water and allow to air dry for one hour. Or, remove any remaining growing medium with a towel or soft brush without washing.

How to get ready: Remove woody stems and set mushrooms aside to be ground into powder.

Small mushrooms can be dried whole, while large ones should be cut into 3/8-inch slices. Save time by purchasing them pre-sliced when they are on sale.

Drying time: between four and eight hours

Temperature: 125°F

Dry consistency: brittle Blanching requirements: not applicable

No oxidizing treatment

How to replenish fluids: Use as a powder or directly in the cooking process.

Consistency following rehydration: Like cooked

1 cup of sliced fresh mushrooms yields 1/2 cup of dehydrated mushrooms, which yields 1 teaspoon of mushroom powder.

Onions (Yellow, White, Red, Sweet)

Onions are a common ingredient in home-cooked meals. Fresh onions can be stored in a pantry for several months if they are hung in a mesh bag or pantyhose. Dehydration is the sole option for long-term storage. Buy them in bulk from August to December, during their peak season, and be sure to give them their own dehydrator time, as their flavor can contaminate other foods.

Clean: Equally treat organic and nonorganic onions. Rinse with cold water and pat dry.

How to get ready: Remove the papery exterior and slice into rings.

Suggestion: 12-inch pieces, sliced, chopped, or minced, depending on the intended application.

Time to dry: 10 to 14 hours

Temperature: 125°F

Durability when dry: Brittle

Exceptions to requirements: Blanch for 15 to 30 seconds in boiling water to accelerate the drying process. For onion powder, there is no need to blanch the onions.

There is no oxidizing treatment, but sweet onions may turn yellow or pink. The color disappears upon rehydration.

How to replenish fluids: Add chopped onion directly to the cooking pot, or grind it into a powder.

Consistency following rehydration: Like fresh

2 cups of fresh onion equals 1 cup of dried onion equals 114 cups of rehydrated onion

Onions can easily fall through the holes in a dehydrator tray. After drying them in 2- to 3-inch-long slices or rings, they can be easily minced in a food processor.

Peaches or Nectarines

Use dried fruit as a substitute for unhealthy snacks. I prefer drying nectarines over peaches because I dislike the process of peeling peaches. Peach cobbler, however, is quite tasty and may convince me to change my mind. Also delicious when cooked, pureed, and incorporated into fruit leather. Try the Honey Peach BBQ Sauce for an additional twist (page 87).

For nonorganic peaches and nectarines, please refer to page 28 for cleaning instructions. Wash organic produce with warm water and pat dry.

How to get ready: Peel if desired. Remove pit.

Recommended thickness: Quarter or cut into eighths. Lie flat on dehydrator sheets without touching.

Drying time: ten to fifteen hours

Temperature: 125°F

Texture when dry: Leathery

To remove the skin from peaches, blanch them in boiling water for one minute, or until the skin blisters.

Oxidizing treatment: Use lemon juice or ascorbic acid.

How to replenish fluids: Pour boiling water over the dried fruits until they are just covered and allow them to soak for 30 minutes, or until they reach the desired consistency.

Consistency following rehydration: Firm, like fresh

2 cups fresh nectarines or peaches = 1 cup dried nectarines or peaches = 114 cups rehydrated nectarines or peaches

Pears

Pears can be rehydrated and made into a flavorful spiced butter (try Slow Cooker Spiced Pear Butter on page 88), or they can be used fresh to make fruit leather.

For cleaning non-organic pears, please refer to page 28. Wash organic peaches with lukewarm water and pat dry.

How to get ready: Remove stems and, if desired, peel. Core and seeds should be sliced and removed.

Recommended thickness: halves, fourths, and eighths

Depending on slice thickness, drying time is between 12 and 24 hours.

Temperature: 125°F

Texture when dry: Leathery

Requirements for blanching: Blanch for two minutes in lieu of oxidizing treatment.

If not blanching, use an ascorbic dip to prevent browning as part of an oxidizing treatment.

How to replenish fluids: Just cover the dried pears with boiling water and let them soak for 30 minutes. Add additional water if necessary.

Consistency following rehydration: as freshly cooked

2 cups of fresh pears equals 1 cup of dried pears equals 112 cups of rehydrated pears

Peas and Chickpeas

Peas are an excellent addition to a food storage program. Each cup contains minimal fat and eight grams of protein. If you purchase frozen peas, you can add them directly to the dehydrator trays and skip the entire preparation process. If you don't mind the taste, canned peas are another quick option.

Clean: Fresh organic and nonorganic peas are peeled and washed in warm water; canned peas are drained and rinsed, and frozen peas are added directly to trays.

How to get ready: Remove peas from their shells.

Not recommended thickness: N/A

Drying time: eight to twelve hours

Temperature: 125°F

Hard consistency when dry

Requirements for blanching: Steam or boil fresh peas for four minutes.

No oxidizing treatment

How to replenish fluids: Add to soup or stew directly, or cover and soak for one hour in cool water.

Consistency following rehydration: Like fresh

3 cups fresh peas equal 1 cup dried peas, which yields 3 cups rehydrated peas.

Peanut (Raw)

Raw, unshelled peanuts that have been appropriately cured can be stored in airtight containers for up to one year. Follow the below instructions to prepare them for drying. Once the peanuts have been prepared for dehydration, you can prepare roasted peanuts and Homemade Roasted Peanut Butter (page 89).

How to prepare and clean: For 12 to 24 hours, soak 4 cups of raw peanuts in warm water with 1 tablespoon of kosher or sea salt. Rinse and drain. Spread in a single layer onto dehydrator sheets. Turn nuts a minimum of once during processing.

Not recommended thickness: N/A

Drying time: twelve to twenty-four hours

Temperature: 155°F

Durability when dry: Brittle

Non-existent requirements for blanching

No oxidizing treatment

Not applicable; roast for snacking and making nut butter.

Nonexistent consistency when rehydrated

4 cups of raw peanuts equals 4 cups of dehydrated peanuts equals 4 cups of rehydrated peanuts

Peppers (Hot, Sweet)

Each year, we produce as many of these as possible. They dehydrate beautifully and are suitable for long-term storage in the pantry. We add diced peppers to our eggs in the morning: Add a handful of peppers to a 10-inch skillet and cover with water. Simmer the water until it has evaporated, and then cook the eggs as usual.

For non-organic peppers, please refer to page 28 for cleaning instructions. Wash and pat dry organic peppers with warm water.

How to get ready: Wash, stem, and core the fruit. Take out the pulp and seeds. Guard your eyes and hands when cutting hot peppers.

Suggestion: 38-inch disks or 1/2-inch dice

Drying time: eight to twelve hours

Temperature: 125°F

Dry consistency: leathery to brittle

Non-existent requirements for blanching

No oxidizing treatment

How to replenish fluids: Soak one cup of dried pepper in two cups of water for one hour, then drain. Alternatively, simmer peppers in water for 10 to 15 minutes.

Consistency following rehydration: as freshly cooked

2 cups of fresh peppers equals 1 cup of dried peppers equals 112 cups of rehydrated peppers

Pineapple

We frequently use pineapple in our morning smoothies, and when it is in season and reasonably priced, fresh pineapple is a treat. If you cannot find fresh pineapple, look for fruit packed in its own juice that is frozen or canned when it goes on sale. When you make it yourself, you control the sugar content. Add pineapple powder to smoothies, consume it dry as a snack, or rehydrate it for a deliciously refreshing treat. Try the low-fat pineapple cake on page 131 for a delectable dessert.

Clean: Fresh organic or nonorganic pineapple must be washed and dried in warm water.

How to get ready: Remove the top and bottom, cut the flesh into quarters, and remove the core and tough skin.

The recommended thickness is 12-inch cubes, 14-inch slices, or crushed. Maintain uniformity on the trays by grouping similar sizes together.

Drying time: eight to sixteen hours, depending on cut size.

Temperature: 125 to 135 degrees Fahrenheit

Durability when dry: Brittle

Non-existent requirements for blanching

No oxidizing treatment

How to replenish fluids: Soak until swollen in cool water.

Consistency following rehydration: Like fresh

2 cups of fresh pineapple is equal to 1 cup of dehydrated pineapple, 112 cups of rehydrated pineapple, and 14 cup of pineapple powder.

Plums

Once upon a time, our family had a plum tree that was completely unappreciated. We did not realize the tree's potential until years after we had it removed, despite the fact that it continued to produce fruit year after year. What a waste that we missed so much jam! Use extremely ripe plums to make the sweetest prunes.

For nonorganic plums, please refer to page 28 for cleaning instructions. Warm water is used to clean organic plums, which are then dried.

How to get ready: Cut the plum in half or quarters and remove the pit. Place plums on trays, skin side down and separate.

Use quarters, which dry faster than halves, as the suggested thickness.

Drying time: 24 hours or more

Temperature: 125°F

Dry consistency: leathery and malleable

To soften the skin, blanch vegetables in boiling water for 30 seconds.

Use lemon juice or ascorbic acid, if desired, for oxidizing lighter-colored fruit.

How to replenish fluids: Bring dried plums and water to a boil in a saucepan. Cover, reduce heat, and simmer for 10 minutes, or until the vegetables are extremely tender.

Consistency following rehydration: Like cooked

2 cups fresh plums equal 1 cup dried plums, which yields 112 cups rehydrated plums.

Make prune powder. If you plan to powder the plums and use the powder in smoothies, cut the fruit into smaller pieces.

Potatoes

In addition to being a pantry staple, potatoes are so versatile that you should never be without them. The humble potato can be stored for four to six months in a properly ventilated root cellar; however, few of us have access to a root cellar. Dehydrate the potatoes for up to five years of long-term storage. Before dehydrating, I find it best to have a purpose in mind: Does the final recipe require slices, shreds, or cubes? Most recipes call for shredded potatoes; try Hash Brown Mix in a Jar on page 121.

Any potato variety can be dehydrated. However, potatoes with waxy skin, such as yellow, white, and red varieties, may dry and rehydrate the best. When using frozen potatoes, it is not necessary to blanch them before dehydrating them.

After dehydration, you may observe that the potato's center has turned black. This occurs when the exterior dries faster than the interior. These potatoes are still edible, but long-term storage is not advised.

Clean: Scrub organic and conventional potatoes with hot water and a vegetable brush.

How to get ready: Keep peel for nutritional value. Process the cooked food into slices, cubes, or shreds.

Suggestions for thickness: 18-inch rounds, 13-inch cubes, and shreds

Time to dry: 8 to 16 hours

Temperature: 125 to 135 degrees Fahrenheit

Durability when dry: brittle and translucent

Exceptions to requirements: Boil for five to six minutes, or until a knife can be partially inserted into the potato.

Oxidizing treatment: Use lemon juice or ascorbic acid to marinate white potatoes.

How to replenish fluids: Add directly to soup or stew, along with additional water, or soak for 30 minutes in hot water.

Consistency following rehydration: Like fresh

2 cups of fresh diced potatoes yield 1 cup of dried potatoes, which yields 114 cups of rehydrated potatoes.

Raspberries and Blackberries

In the Pacific Northwest, summer berries are known as loganberry, blackberry, salmonberry, boysenberry, and marionberry. If you live in berry country, you know that these fruits are most delicious when purchased directly from the farmer. Now that I reside in Texas, these berries are expensive and inferior in quality. I prefer to purchase frozen berries as opposed to store-bought berries. Next time I return to Oregon in July, I will dehydrate countless batches of berries and ship them home via FedEx!

Clean: For non-organic berries, refer to page 28 for cleaning instructions. If at all possible, avoid washing these delicate berries. Before dehydrating, berries must be completely air-dried, as wet berries will lose their shape during the drying process.

How to get ready: Dry berries on all sides by placing them on their flat ends. Utilize dehydrator sheets; as they dry, they will drip, leaving juice on the trays below.

Recommended thickness: Dry overall

Drying time: 15 to 20 hours, size dependent

Temperature: 125°F

Dry consistency: brittle or pulverized to a powder

Non-existent requirements for blanching

No oxidizing treatment

How to replenish fluids: Mist with a spray bottle for shape retention; simmer in juice or water for pie filling. Produce berry powder for use in smoothies.

Consistency following rehydration: as freshly cooked

2 cups of fresh berries equals 1 cup of dried berries equals 114 cups of rehydrated berries

Rhubarb

Rhubarb, once a kitchen garden staple, is experiencing a surge in popularity as a home garden crop. It thrives in regions where the ground freezes during the winter. Both the roots and leaves are toxic and should not be consumed. The tender stalks are frequently combined with berries and used to make jam, pies, and condiment sauces.

For cleaning non-organic rhubarb, refer to the cleaning instructions on page 28. Wash organic rhubarb with warm water and pat dry thoroughly.

How to get ready: Leave the leaves behind, then cut the stem into pieces of equal size.

Recommended thickness: half-inch to one-inch pieces

Drying time: eight to twelve hours

Temperature: 135°F

Durability when dry: Brittle

Exceptions to requirements: Steam vegetables for five minutes or boil for one minute until tender. Use ice water to cool off.

No oxidizing treatment

How to rehydrate: Soak until plump in hot water.

Consistency following rehydration: Like fresh

212 cups of fresh rhubarb yields 1 cup of dried rhubarb and 112 cups of rehydrated rhubarb.

Spinach

Similarly to preserving lettuce, drying spinach leaves might appear strange. In fact, 1 cup of spinach leaves only yields 1 tablespoon of spinach powder. However, the health benefits of incorporating spinach powder into smoothies, soups, and baked goods make the effort worthwhile. We purchase large quantities of organic spinach from a nearby warehouse club, consume as much as we can, and then dehydrate the remainder. This method makes spinach economical, and no food is wasted.

Clean: For non-organic spinach, refer to page 28 for cleaning instructions. Wash and pat dry organic spinach with cool water.

When preparing for cooking, remove the stems. If powdering, keep intact.

Whole leaves are the recommended thickness.

Four to six hours for drying

Temperature: 110°F

Dry consistency: brittle Blanching requirements: not applicable

No oxidizing treatment

Add 1 cup of dried spinach to 1 cup of water and let it soak for half an hour. Alternately, add directly to a recipe or as a baking powder.

Consistency following rehydration: Like cooked

2 cups of fresh spinach equals 1 cup of dried spinach equals 112 cups of rehydrated spinach equals 1 tablespoon of spinach powder.

Strawberries

Strawberries top the EWG's "Dirty Dozen" list of fruits with the highest concentration of pesticides. Unless you are purchasing organic produce or growing your own, it will be particularly important to thoroughly clean them before drying. If you do not have access to fresh strawberries, frozen strawberries dry exceptionally well, but they do not retain their shape as well as fresh strawberries do after drying.

Clean: For nonorganic strawberries, follow the cleaning tips on page 28. For organic berries, wash with warm water and pat dry lightly.

How to prepare: Remove tops and soft spots.

Suggested thickness: Cut small to medium berries in half. Cut large berries into quarters.

Drying time: 8 to 16 hours

Temperature: 125°F

Consistency when dry: Pliable, dry in center

Blanching requirements: N/A

Oxidizing treatment: Use lemon juice or ascorbic acid, if you'd like, for lighter colored fruit.

How to rehydrate: Soak in hot water or warmed juice for 15 to 20 minutes, or simmer in water on the stovetop until the fruit is plump and has absorbed the water.

Consistency when rehydrated: Plump, but mushy. Best for sauces or shortcake.

Yield: 2½ cups fresh strawberries = 1 cup dried strawberries = 1 cup rehydrated strawberries

Summer Squash

A late-season garden typically contains an abundance of summer squash. Each year, we cultivate traditional zucchini, yellow crookneck, and pattypan, which we then dice or shred for soup. They also produce nutritious chips. The Zucchini Chips on page 106 are so popular that it is difficult to keep them in stock. We vary the spices according to the occasion, and they are prepared without oil, so the calories are minimal.

Clean: For both organic and nonorganic squash, wash using natural soap and warm water, then towel dry.

How to prepare: Cut off the ends, then use a mandoline to cut uniform slices.

Suggested thickness: ⅛- to ¼-inch rounds for chips, or ½-inch cubes

Drying time: 10 to 12 hours for chips, 12 to 18 hours for cubes

Temperature: 125°F

Consistency when dry: Crisp

Blanching requirements: N/A

Oxidizing treatment: N/A

How to rehydrate: Soak in warm water 15 minutes, drop whole into soup, or eat as chips.

Consistency when rehydrated: Like cooked

Yield: 2 cups fresh summer squash = 1 cup dried summer squash = 1½ cups rehydrated summer squash

Sweet Potatoes and Yams

Sweet potatoes are high in beta carotene, magnesium, calcium, potassium, and iron, as well as nutrients E and C. Just what you'd want in a plan for shelf-stable food storage! Three to five weeks in a cool, dark pantry, and two to three months in the fridge. Dehydration increases their shelf life to up to five years. All of these recipes can also be made with yams: Sweet Potato Chips (page 104), Sweet Potato Powder (page 92), and Mashed Sweet Potatoes (page 93).

Clean: Scrub organic and nonorganic sweet potatoes clean with a vegetable brush and warm water, then pat dry.

How to prepare: Leave the skins on for added fiber, or peel and grate, slice, or cube.

Suggested thickness: ⅛-inch round slices; ⅓-inch cubes; shreds. Cut when cold.

Drying time: 8 to 16 hours

Temperature: 125°F

Consistency when dry: Brittle

Blanching requirements: Steam or boil until completely cooked. Cool in refrigerator overnight.

Oxidizing treatment: N/A

How to rehydrate: Add 1 cup dried sweet potatoes to 2 cups boiling water, soak for an hour. Alternatively, add cubes directly to a soup, or eat chips dried.

Consistency when rehydrated: Like freshly cooked

Yield: 2 cups fresh sweet potatoes = 1 cup dried sweet potatoes = 1½ cups rehydrated sweet potatoes

Tomatoes

Everyone desires tomatoes in their emergency food storage. It is the most adaptable fruit that can be preserved. We use tomato pieces that have retained their skin to create a powder. The powder is rehydrated to create a paste and a sauce. When using a water bath canner, blanching and peeling the fruit's skin (which I abhor) is required. However, I find it quicker to simply dry the fruits instead of going through the tedious process.

Clean: For nonorganic tomatoes, follow the cleaning tips. For organic tomatoes, wash with warm water and pat dry.

How to prepare: Optionally, remove the skins by blanching. Core tomatoes and remove tomato ends.

Suggested thickness: Cut stewing or slicing tomatoes into quarters; cut cherry tomatoes in half.

Drying time: 8 to 12 hours

Temperature: 135°F

Consistency when dry: Leathery to brittle

Blanching requirements: Cut an X into the bottom of the tomato with a knife, just deep enough to penetrate the skin. Tomatoes are placed in boiling water. Blanch for twenty to thirty seconds. Remove tomatoes from boiling water using a slotted spoon. Soak tomatoes in ice water. Using a knife, remove the tomato's center. The skin will peel off.

Oxidizing treatment: N/A

How to rehydrate: Cover tomatoes with cool water in a bowl for 30 to 60 minutes, then drain. Alternatively, use a spray bottle to apply a small amount of cool water to each tomato slice. Repeat approximately every 15 minutes until the fruit has plumped up.

Consistency when rehydrated: Soft, like cooked

Yield: 2 cups fresh tomatoes = 1 cup dried tomatoes = 1½ cups rehydrated tomatoes = ⅔ cup tomato powder

These common tomato products can be made with shelf-stable tomato powder:
- *Tomato soup = 1 part tomato powder + 1 part water + 2 parts cream*

- *Tomato paste = Equal amounts tomato powder + water*
- *Tomato sauce = 1 part tomato powder + 3 parts water*
- *Tomato juice = 1 teaspoon tomato powder + ½ cup water*

Watermelon

This snack brings a taste of summer to your diet during the winter. If you can keep it that long, you can store this item for more than a year by placing the dehydrated fruit in the freezer for two weeks to pasteurize it and then vacuum-packing it in serving-size packages with oxygen absorbers. Place the vacuum-packed bags in an opaque container to protect them from direct sunlight.

Clean: The rind of organic and nonorganic watermelon should be washed with soap and warm water, then dried.

How to get ready: Cut the melon into 12-inch thick slices. Separate the meat from the rinds and cut it into 2- to 3-inch pieces. Discard seeds.

Suggested thickness: ½-inch rounds

Drying time: 8 to 12 hours

Temperature: 125°F

Consistency when dry: Like fruit leather

Blanching requirements: N/A

Oxidizing treatment: N/A

How to rehydrate: Not typically rehydrated; eaten as a dry snack.

Consistency when rehydrated: N/A

Yield: 2 cups fresh watermelon = ½ cup dehydrated watermelon = 1½ cups rehydrated watermelon

Winter Squash (Pumpkin, Acorn, Butternut, Delicata)

Winter squash can be stored for many months in a root cellar or a cool, dark area of your pantry, but it deteriorates rapidly below 50 degrees Fahrenheit. Dehydration is a viable option if you produce more than you can store. There are three advantages to preserving your winter squash in a dehydrator: The finished product is lightweight, requires little storage space, and can be stored away from direct light and heat for many years.

Acorn, buttercup, butternut, banana, golden delicious, Hubbard, and sweet meat are winter squash varieties. Pumpkin and other winter squashes can be dehydrated and used in soups and sautés (see Sautéed Winter Squash with Apples on page 116). For pies and other recipes, such as leathers (try Pumpkin Pie Leather on page 100), dried and rehydrated cubes do not work well; it is difficult to achieve the correct consistency due to case hardening, so purees work better. Try making Garlic Creole Spiced Squash Nests using shredded squash that dries well in small nest-like portions (page 118).

Wash organic or nonorganic winter squash with soap and warm water, then pat dry with a towel.

How to get ready: Remove the squash's peel and seeds, then puree or cut into pieces. For pureeing, cut the squash in half lengthwise and cook, cut side down, at 400°F for 30 to 45 minutes, or until completely soft. Puree the fruit pulp in a bowl using an immersion blender. Spread the pulp onto Paraflexx sheets no thicker than 14 inch.

Cut into 14-inch cubes or 14-inch-thick strips that are 1 to 2 inches long. Alternately, puree or shred the ingredients.

Drying time: 8 to 12 hours

Temperature: 140°F for two to three hours, then reduce temperature to 130°F and continue drying for three to six hours, or until squash is tough and brittle.

Consistency when dry: Brittle

Blanching requirements: Boil for three minutes.

Oxidizing treatment: N/A

How to rehydrate: Soak the dehydrated squash pieces for 30 minutes in boiling water before draining and continuing with the recipe. Save the liquid from soaking to use in soups. Place bird's nest fragments in boiling water. Or, for fruit leather, pour boiling water over 1-inch squares of fruit and mix until the desired consistency is reached.

Consistency when rehydrated: Like freshly blanched

Yield: 2 12 cups fresh winter squash equals 1 cup dried winter squash which rehydrates to 2 cups fresh winter squash.

CHAPTER 10: DELICIOUS DEHYDRATOR RECIPES

Blueberry Basil Syrup

Creating a syrup with dehydrated fruit is a fantastic way to extend the shelf life of your pantry's contents. In addition, who does not enjoy warm blueberries on Sunday morning pancakes? You can substitute any fruit for blueberries, omit or replace the herbs in this recipe, or use store-bought juice instead of juicing fresh fruit. It is that adaptable!

Yield: 3 cups

Prep time: 10 minutes

Cook time: 10 minutes

¼ cup dried basil leaves

2 cups dehydrated blueberries

2 cups sugar

⅛ teaspoon ascorbic acid

1. To make blueberry juice, rehydrate the blueberries in 2½ cups of water in a nonreactive saucepan. Bring to a boil and simmer for 10 minutes, mashing the fruit as it cooks and stirring constantly. Strain the mixture to remove the berries. Set aside berries.
2. Bring the blueberry juice, sugar, and basil leaves to a full boil in a saucepan. Reduce the heat and simmer the ingredients for 5 minutes. Remove any foam.
3. Remove pan from heat and strain basil leaves.
4. If you prefer blueberry chunks in your syrup, you may return the strained syrup to the saucepan and add the blueberries. Simmer for 2 minutes.
5. Remove the saucepan from the heat and stir in the ascorbic acid. Stir to combine ingredients.
6. Pour the completed syrup into sterile jars, then seal and label them. This syrup can be used immediately or stored in bottles with a swing-top cap for up to one year if ascorbic acid is added, or for six months if it is not. Reducing the amount of sugar will reduce the product's shelf life. Any opened bottles can be stored in the refrigerator for up to two weeks.

Pectin with Citrus Pith

Citrus dehydration can result in an abundance of pith, which is rich in pectin (the white, bitter substance beneath the flavorful rind). Most methods of food preservation involve composting the pith, but you can use it to make homemade pectin to thicken jam and jelly. You can freeze small amounts of pith until you have enough for a batch from any citrus fruit. Seeking citrus with abundant pith? It's all about the thickness of the skin. Citrus fruits with thick skin will have a great deal of pith inside.

Yield: 2 cups

Prep time: 5 minutes

Cook time: 20 minutes, plus rest time

> ½ pound citrus pith and seeds
>
> ¼ cup citrus juice, such as lemon

1. Utilize a vegetable peeler to remove the fruit's skin. Save the skin for dehydrating.
2. Employ a vegetable peeler to eliminate the pith. Cut the pith into small pieces and set it aside with the seeds.
3. Add pith, seeds, and citrus juice to a nonreactive pot of medium size. Allow pot to rest for one hour.
4. Add 2 cups of water and let it sit for an additional hour.
5. Bring the pot's contents to a boil over high heat. Reduce the heat and simmer for fifteen minutes. Temperature at room temperature
6. The mixture should be placed in a jelly bag and allowed to drain. Press to extract juice.
7. Keep any excess pectin in the freezer.

Pink Grapefruit Jelly

Yield: 2 cups

Prep time: 15 minutes

Cook time: 30 minutes

> 4 handfuls dehydrated pink grapefruit peels or rounds
>
> 2 cups cool water
>
> 1 ½ cups sugar

1. Place grapefruit peels or rounds in a large bowl and cover with cool water for approximately fifteen minutes, or until plump. Drain and reserve the liquid from the grapefruit.
2. The rehydrated grapefruit must be chopped into small pieces.
3. Add half a pound of the grapefruit pieces, along with the reserved water and sugar, to a nonreactive pot. If necessary, add enough water to cover the grapefruit pieces. Boil for 30 minutes until thoroughly cooked.
4. The liquid should be drained through a jelly bag. Allow to cool slightly, then squeeze out all liquid.

Ginger and Lemon Infused Honey

For this recipe, dried herbs are recommended. To reduce the risk of introducing bacteria into the honey, you must thoroughly wash and dry any fresh herbs or spices you intend to use. When you feel a cold coming on, use this recipe as it is very soothing.

Yield: 1 cup

Prep time: 5 minutes, plus 2-week wait time

- 1 tablespoon dried ginger
- 1 teaspoon dried citrus peel
- 1 cup raw, unfiltered, unpasteurized honey, slightly warmed

1. Chop the dried ginger and citrus in a coffee grinder to release their fragrant flavors.
2. Place the ginger and citrus in a tea bag or square of cheesecloth and secure the bag/square with string so that it remains closed. It is nearly impossible to separate dried herbs from honey.
3. Pour three-quarters of the slightly warmed honey over the herb bag in a pint jar. Using a chopstick or skewer, stir the honey to eliminate air bubbles and ensure that the herb bag is completely saturated.
4. Fill the jar to the top with the remaining honey. Close the lid securely. Place the jar out of direct sunlight in a location where you can observe the process.
5. Give the flavors two weeks to infuse. In order to prevent the spice bag from rising to the surface, turn the jar upside down. This will keep the flavors submerged and lightly combine the honey.
6. After two weeks, remove the tea bag and store the honey for up to one year in the pantry.

Honey Peach BBQ Sauce

In the final minutes of grilling, brush this sweet and spicy sauce over chicken or pork. It becomes more viscous as it cools. Use less chipotle for a sauce with less heat.

Yield: 1 cup

Prep time: 30 minutes

Cook time: 20 minutes

- ¼ teaspoon ground cumin
- pinch of allspice
- ¼ cup honey
- 16 slices dehydrated peaches or 1 cup fresh sliced peaches

2 teaspoons olive oil

1 cup chopped onion

1 teaspoon salt

1 teaspoon chipotle powder

4 teaspoons apple cider vinegar

1. Soak peaches for 30 minutes in a large bowl filled with warm water. Remove and dispose of the soaking liquid. Chop the rehydrated peaches roughly. and set aside.
2. Apply olive oil to the bottom of a medium saucepan. Add onions and cook over medium heat until softened and beginning to brown, about 5 minutes.
3. Add salt, chipotle, cumin, and allspice and cook for 30 seconds, or until the spices smell fragrant.
4. Stir in the rehydrated peaches, honey, and vinegar to coat.
5. Cover the saucepan, increase the heat to medium-high, and cook the peaches for 15 minutes, or until they are completely soft and breaking down.
6. Transfer to a blender or use an immersion blender to puree. Add more apple cider vinegar to thin out the sauce.

Slow Cooker Spiced Pear Butter

Alternately, you can prepare the recipe with fresh pears and dehydrate the end result. To reconstitute butter, add small amounts of boiling water until the desired consistency is reached.

Yield: 3 cups

Prep time: 1 hour

Cook time: 4 to 8 hours

1 tablespoon cinnamon

1 teaspoon ground ginger

1 pound dehydrated pear sections (approximately 10 fresh pears)

¼ cup brown sugar

½ teaspoon ground nutmeg

1. Add the dehydrated pears and enough water to cover them to a slow cooker. Cook on low for one hour with the lid removed, until the pears rehydrate.
2. Stir the remaining ingredients together in the slow cooker, then cover.
3. Four hours on high or six to eight hours on low.
4. Use an immersion blender to puree the mixture, or transfer in small batches to a blender and puree.
5. Keep refrigerated for up to three weeks.

Homemade Roasted Peanut Butter

Enjoy this peanut butter on its own, or experiment by blending in dark chocolate powder, banana chips, white chocolate chips, maple, or coconut. Did you know that raw peanuts have a bean-like flavor? Before being roasted for peanut butter, raw peanuts must be soaked and dehydrated for optimal flavor.

Yield: ½ cup

Prep time: 20 minutes

Cook time: 5 minutes

- 2 cups dehydrated peanuts
- honey, to taste

1. Preheat oven to 300 degrees Fahrenheit.
2. Spread peanuts on a baking sheet to a maximum thickness of half an inch. Roast for 20 minutes. When properly roasted, they will be slightly browned and have the flavor of peanuts, which is pleasant, nutty, and distinct from that of beans.
3. In a food processor, grind the roasted peanuts for approximately 5 minutes, or until butter forms. Add honey to taste and process for an additional minute until the desired consistency is reached. Extra vegetable or peanut oil can be added to peanut butter to thin it out.

Creamy Cucumber Salad Dressing

Yield: 2 cups

Prep time: 15 minutes

- 1 tablespoon light mayonnaise
- 1 tablespoon lemon juice
- 1 cup dehydrated cucumber chips
- ½ cup dehydrated green onions
- ½ teaspoon dried garlic
- ¾ cup light sour cream
- 1 teaspoon dried dill weed, basil, or parsley

1. Cucumber chips and onions should be soaked in cool water for 15 minutes in a large bowl. Remove and dispose of the soaking liquid.
2. Blend or process the rehydrated vegetables and remaining ingredients until smooth in a blender or small food processor.
3. If the dressing needs to be diluted, add a splash of milk.

Tomato Powder

The more dry your tomatoes are, the simpler it will be to powder them. If you plan to turn your dried tomatoes into a powder, you may need to dehydrate them for an additional hour or two beyond what is recommended on page 78. The duration of the process is entirely dependent on the quality of the grinder you use; I've discovered that a coffee grinder works best. However, it is worthwhile to keep a few cups of tomato powder on hand for cooking emergencies.

Yield: ⅔ cup

Prep time: 5 minutes

1 cup dehydrated tomatoes, divided

1. In 1/4-cup increments, pulverize dehydrated tomatoes in a food processor, blender, or coffee grinder until powdery.
2. Transfer to a mesh strainer and agitate with a spatula until the powder falls through the mesh.

Sweet Potato Powder

Using boiling water to rehydrate sweet potato powder produces "instant" mashed sweet potatoes. It is ideal for making baby food or preparing a healthy side dish. Refrigerate the sweet potato powder in a jar for up to one month. Include a 100cc oxygen absorber in the jar or vacuum-seal the jar with a FoodSaver jar attachment to extend storage time. Refrigerate for three months maximum.

Yield: 2 cups mash, ½ cup powder

Prep time: 60 minutes

Cook time: 5 to 8 hours

2 pounds sweet potatoes

1. Peel or leave the skins on sweet potatoes for added nutritional value. Reduced to thin strips. Boil sweet potatoes for 10 to 15 minutes, or until tender, then drain and reserve cooking liquid. Alternately, bake whole and then cut into strips after cooking.
2. Sweet potatoes are mashed to a smooth consistency. If necessary, thin with water, preferably cooking liquid.
3. Spread half a cup of potato mash on each Paraflexx sheet, tray lined with plastic wrap, or fruit leather sheet. Extremely thin.
4. Dry at 135 degrees Fahrenheit for four to six hours. Turn the sweet potato sheets over when the top is dry, remove the tray wrap, and dry the underside for an additional 1 to 2 hours if necessary.
5. When the sweet potato sheets are crisp and the product crumbles, the drying process is

complete.

6. Blend or process the dehydrated sweet potato bark into a powder in a blender or food processor.

Other Uses for Sweet Potato Powder

- *Prepare instant mashed sweet potatoes by slowly adding hot water to sweet potato powder until a thick mashed potato consistency is achieved. Add sugar and seasonings as necessary.*
- *Replace 12 cup of white flour with sweet potato flour when preparing biscuits.*
- *Sweet potato powder can be added to morning smoothies.*
- *Combine 1 tablespoon of sweet potato powder, 12 cup of quick oats, and 1 cup of boiling water to make morning porridge.*

Celery Salt

This salt can be used for everyday cooking, canning, and even fermentation. Be sure to adjust the salt content of your recipe. Under normal pantry conditions, celery salt will last at least one year when stored in a canning jar.

Yield: 1 cup

Prep time: 5 minutes

½ cup dried celery stalks and leaves

½ cup kosher salt, plus more as needed

1. Utilize a coffee grinder or food processor to finely grind the celery.
2. Add the kosher salt and process the mixture in short bursts for one minute, until the desired consistency is achieved. Adjust the proportions of salt and celery to your liking.

Green Powder Blend

If you have extra greens in the crisper drawer, you should not throw them away. Any greens will do. Using these leftovers to create a green powder blend is simple and will be just as healthy as eating fresh greens. You can add more greens to your diet by adding the powder to smoothies. You can store your favorite vegetables as individual powders or create a custom blend.

Yield: 2 cups powder

Prep time: 5 minutes

Cook time: 4 to 8 hours

6 cups fresh spinach leaves

fresh kale leaves

1. Before dehydrating, it is not necessary to trim the vegetable leaves; however, you may wish to remove tough ribs, stems, and seeds.
2. Dry vegetables at 100 degrees Fahrenheit and begin checking for dryness after four hours. Depending on the size and thickness of the leaves, this could take up to eight hours.
3. Once the leaves are dry, rub them between your hands to break them up. Utilize a food processor, blender, or coffee grinder to reduce the greens to powder form. Powder is strained through a sieve. Re-blend any large chunks until the entire mixture is powdered.

Shredded Coconut

You must really enjoy fresh coconut to go to the trouble of cracking, peeling, and shredding it! For fine or regular shreds, use a grater with small or medium holes, a slicer for coconut chips, or a vegetable peeler for thicker chips.

Yield: 2 to 3 cups

Prep time: 20 minutes

Cook time: 6 to 10 hours

1 small fresh coconut, husked

1. Make a hole in the coconut's top and drain the milk.
2. Break the coconut in half along the center line using a hammer. Remove the tough outer layer.
3. Using a vegetable peeler or a sharp knife, remove the soft outer membrane.
4. Variously grate the fresh coconut meat.
5. Dry small and medium shreds on a dehydrator tray for 6 to 8 hours at 110 degrees Fahrenheit. The completion of thick coconut shreds may take up to 10 hours.

Coconut Flour

Occasionally, it will be necessary to increase the amount of liquid in a coconut flour-based recipe. Due to its affinity for water, coconut flour will absorb additional liquid in a recipe. Flour can be stored for up to six months in an airtight container in a dark, cool cabinet.

Yield: ½ cup

Prep time: 5 minutes

Cook time: 2 to 4 hours

1 cup Shredded Coconut (page 96)

2 cups water

1. Combine the shredded coconut and 2 cups of water in a blender. Process the coconut on high until it is finely chopped.
2. To drink the milk, strain it through a jelly bag and save it.
3. Spread the pulp on a dehydrator Paraflexx sheet and dry it at 110 degrees Fahrenheit for two to four hours.
4. Process the dehydrated pulp into a fine powder once it has dried. This coconut flour will be lower in fat and will require more liquid or eggs when used in cooking.

Strawberry Banana Rolls

Fruit leather is typically consumed as a snack, but it can also be rehydrated for use in pie fillings and dessert toppings, or as a soup base with vegetables, bouillon, and seasonings. Use these as snacks for your backpack or emergency kit.

Yield: 3 large trays, 24 rolls

Prep time: 10 minutes

Cook time: 6 to 8 hours

honey (optional)

2 pounds strawberries, hulled

3 medium-size ripe bananas

water or fruit juice, as needed

1. Quarter the strawberries and add them to a blender.
2. Add bananas that have been cut into 2-inch pieces to the blender.
3. Adding honey to taste is optional.
4. Following the no-cook fruit leather instructions on page 38, puree the fruit until smooth. As necessary, add water or juice in 1-tablespoon increments to thin the mixture.
5. Cover the trays of a dehydrator with a fruit leather tray or plastic wrap. Spoon the mixture onto dehydrator trays in equal portions. Cover with plastic wrap or tray covers. Dry at 125 degrees Fahrenheit for six to eight hours.

Cinnamon Apple Leather

Yield: 4 large trays, 36 rolls

Prep time: 40 minutes

Cook time: 6 to 10 hours

ground cinnamon, to taste

2 tablespoons lemon juice

8 sweet apples, peeled and cored

1 cup water

sugar, to taste (optional)

1. Finely dice the apples. Apples and water are added to a large pot. Cover and simmer on low heat for fifteen minutes.
2. If desired, mash the apples in a pot and add cinnamon, lemon juice, and sugar. Simmer for 10 minutes.
3. Once mixture has cooled, pass apples through a blender or food mill in small batches until a consistent puree forms.
4. Cover the trays of a dehydrator with a fruit leather tray or plastic wrap. Spread the puree in a 14-inch-thick layer on dehydrator trays. Cover with plastic wrap or tray covers. Dry at 125 degrees Fahrenheit for six to ten hours.

Pumpkin Pie Leather

Yield: 3 large trays, 24 rolls

Prep time: 5 to 20 minutes if using canned pumpkin; 40 to 60 minutes for fresh pumpkin

Cook time: 8 to 10 hours

2 teaspoons ground cinnamon

½ teaspoon ground nutmeg

½ teaspoon powdered cloves

1 (29-ounce) can pumpkin or 3 cups fresh pumpkin, cooked and pureed

¼ cup honey

¼ cup applesauce

½ teaspoon ground ginger

1. In a large bowl, combine all the ingredients until a puree is formed.
2. Cover the trays of a dehydrator with a fruit leather tray or plastic wrap. Spread the puree in a 14-inch-thick layer on dehydrator trays. Cover with plastic wrap or tray covers. Dry at 130 degrees Fahrenheit for eight to ten hours.

Pizza Blend Tomato Leather

If you have extra tomatoes after the harvest, consider making pizza-flavored leather. You can make this tomato leather plain and rehydrate it to make sauce, or you can add flavor with the Pizza Seasoning Blend listed below.

Yield: 2 large trays, 16 rolls

Prep time: 40 minutes

Cook time: 8 to 12 hours

1 pound tomatoes, cored and quartered

½ tablespoon Pizza Seasoning Blend (optional)

1. Cook the tomatoes for 15 to 20 minutes in a medium saucepan covered over low heat. Take the dish off the heat and let it cool for a few minutes.
2. Blend or process the cooked tomatoes until smooth in a blender or food processor. If desired, add seasoning and blend.
3. Return the puree to the saucepan and heat until the water has evaporated and the sauce has thickened, or until the sauce has thickened and the water has evaporated.
4. Cover the trays of a dehydrator with a fruit leather tray or plastic wrap. Spread tomato puree in a 14-inch-thick layer on dehydrator trays. Cover with plastic wrap or tray covers. Dry at 135 degrees Fahrenheit for eight to twelve hours.

Mixed Vegetable Leather

Yield: 1 large tray, 8 rolls

Prep time: 40 minutes

Cook time: 4 to 8 hours

¼ cup chopped celery

1 sprig basil

2 cups tomatoes, cored and cut into chunks

1 small onion, chopped

salt, to taste

1. Cook the ingredients for 15 to 20 minutes in a covered medium saucepan over low heat. Take the dish off the heat and let it cool for a few minutes.
2. Blend the ingredients in a blender until smooth.
3. Return the puree to the saucepan and heat until the water has evaporated and the sauce has thickened, or until the sauce has thickened and the water has evaporated.
4. Cover the trays of a dehydrator with a fruit leather tray or plastic wrap. Spread the puree in a 14-inch-thick layer on dehydrator trays. Cover with plastic wrap or tray covers. Dry at 135 degrees Fahrenheit until pliable (for a wrap), approximately four hours, or until crisp (for use in soups and casseroles), six to eight hours.

Tomato Wraps

This vegan leather does not need to be cooked. Use as a snack wrap or to encase meat and cheese. Try this method with carrot, cucumber, spinach, zucchini, yellow squash, or eggplant. Try adding spices, peppers, onions, garlic, ground flaxseed, or chia seed.

Yield: 2 large trays, 6 wraps

Prep time: 5 minutes

Cook time: 4 hours

2 pounds tomatoes, cored and chopped

seasonings, to taste

1. Blend or process the fresh tomatoes until smooth in a blender or food processor.
2. Add seasonings to taste.
3. Cover the trays of a dehydrator with a fruit leather tray or plastic wrap. Spread the puree in a 14-inch-thick layer on dehydrator trays. Cover with plastic wrap or tray covers. Dry at 125°F for four hours, or until pliable and easily removable from the trays, but not crisp.

Sweet Potato Chips

Sweet potato chips are a healthy alternative to store-bought potato chips that my family enjoys. I disagree with those who recommend making these chips without cooking the potatoes. Without precooking, the chips will be inedible and as hard as a rock. Season chips with your preferred seasonings. Consider using sugar, cinnamon, and nutmeg; salt, black pepper, and onion powder; or salt and smoked paprika. You can also leave the chips uncoated and rehydrate them for use in soups and stews.

Yield: 6 cups

Prep time: 15 minutes

Cook time: 4 to 8 hours

4 large sweet potatoes

1. Peel or leave potato skins on for added nutritional value.
2. Cut each potato into 1/8-inch-thick rounds using a mandoline.
3. Add the rounds to a large pot of boiling water and cook for approximately 10 minutes, or until tender. Drain and discard liquid. They should retain their shape when handled without being overcooked.
4. Place moist rounds of sweet potato on dehydrator trays. They are not to touch.
5. Sprinkle chips with salt and seasonings (optional).

6. Dry at 125 degrees Fahrenheit for four to eight hours, or until the chips are crisp and the centers are cooked.

Kale Chips

Yield: 2 cups

Prep time: 5 minutes

Cook time: 4 to 6 hours

1 tablespoon olive oil or apple cider vinegar

1 bunch kale, stems removed

seasoning, as desired

1. The kale leaves should be cut into 2- to 3-inch strips.
2. Lightly brush the kale with olive oil or use apple cider vinegar as a low-calorie alternative. This provides something for the seasoning to adhere to.
3. Sprinkle the kale with the seasoning of your choosing.
4. Spread the seasoned kale onto dehydrator trays and dry at 125 degrees Fahrenheit for four to six hours, or until crisp.

Zucchini Chips

Yield: 5 cups

Prep time: 15 minutes

Cook time: 10 to 12 hours

pepper, to taste

4 medium zucchini squash

¼ cup apple cider vinegar

salt, to taste

chili powder, to taste

1. Thinly slice the zucchini into rounds. It is best to maintain the same thickness for uniform drying. Experiment with a crinkle cut slicing blade that creates ridges in the chips; the ridges tend to provide spices with a larger surface area to adhere to.
2. Place apple cider vinegar, salt, pepper, and chili powder in a nonreactive bowl with a wide bottom. Stir until thoroughly mixed.
3. Add a handful of raw chips to the bowl and toss them with the vinegar and spice mixture until they are evenly coated. Separate any pieces that have adhered together and ensure that each slice of zucchini is coated with the spices.

4. Spread the chips across the dehydrator trays. They may come in contact but should not overlap.
5. Dry at 135 degrees Fahrenheit for 10 to 12 hours. If your dehydrator heats from the bottom, you may need to reposition the trays halfway through the drying cycle. After 5 hours, invert the upper trays so that the chips are evenly dried.

Yield: 1½ cups

2 tablespoons onion powder

2 tablespoons dried oregano

1 tablespoon dried thyme

¼ cup garlic powder

¼ cup kosher or sea salt

½ cup paprika

2 tablespoons pepper

1 tablespoon cayenne powder (optional)

1. In a jar with sufficient space for shaking, combine all the ingredients.

Dehydrated Refrigerator Pickles

Yield: 1 pint

Prep time: 5 minutes

Cook time: At least 24-hour wait time

¼ teaspoon dill seed

⅛ teaspoon red pepper flakes

1 cup vinegar

1 cup water

1½ tablespoons pickling salt or kosher salt

1 garlic clove, smashed

1½ cups dehydrated cucumber slices or spears

1. In a small saucepan over high heat, combine vinegar, water, and salt to prepare the brine. Bring to a rolling boil, then remove and allow to cool immediately.
2. In a pint-sized canning jar, combine the garlic, dill seed, red pepper flakes, and dehydrated cucumber slices.
3. Pour the cooled brine over the cucumbers to within 12 inch of the top of the jar. You may

not utilize all of the brine.

4. Refrigerate at least 24 hours prior to consumption. Overnight, the cucumbers will swell and magically transform into pickles.

My Classic Beef Jerky

Yield: ¾ pound

Prep time: 15 minutes, plus overnight

Cook time: 5 to 8 hours

1 tablespoon barbecue sauce

½ teaspoon pepper

½ teaspoon salt

½ teaspoon onion

1 ½ pounds lean beef

2 cups white vinegar

¼ cup soy sauce

⅓ cup Worcestershire sauce

½ teaspoon garlic

1. Slice the beef into 14-inch slices.
2. In a medium bowl, pre-treat the beef slices for 10 minutes with the white vinegar. Remove and dispose of the white vinegar.
3. Place the beef slices and brine ingredients in a gallon-sized zipper bag. If necessary, add water to completely cover the meat. Soak in the refrigerator overnight.
4. The following day, drain the brine, separate the meat pieces, and dehydrate them at 160°F for 5 to 8 hours until they are crisp but pliable.

Beef Steak Jerky

Yield: ¾ pound

Prep time: 15 minutes, plus overnight

Cook time: 5 to 8 hours

1 tablespoon Steak Seasoning Blend (see recipe below)

1 teaspoon fresh garlic

1 ½ pounds lean beef

2 cups white vinegar

¼ cup balsamic vinegar

⅓ cup Worcestershire sauce

1 tablespoon molasses

1 teaspoon onion powder

1. Cut beef into 14-inch thick slices.
2. In a medium bowl, marinate beef slices in white vinegar for 10 minutes. Drain the white vinegar and dispose of it.
3. Add the beef slices and brine ingredients to a 1-gallon resealable plastic bag. If needed, add water to cover the meat completely. Refrigerate overnight to soak.
4. The following day, drain the brine, lay out the meat so that no pieces are touching, and dehydrate at 160°F for 5 to 8 hours, or until crisp but flexible.

Cauliflower Soup

Yield: 6 cups

Prep time: 40 minutes

Cook time: 15 minutes

⅛ cup quinoa

4 cups vegetable stock

pepper, to taste

salt, to taste

2 cups dehydrated cauliflower

⅛ cup dehydrated onion

⅛ cup dehydrated celery

2 slices dehydrated garlic

2½ cups water

seasoning, to taste

1. Cover cauliflower, onion, celery, and garlic with 2½ cups boiling water in a large bowl. Soak vegetables for about 30 minutes, or until nearly rehydrated. Remove and dispose of the soaking liquid.
2. Add the vegetables, quinoa, vegetable stock, salt, pepper, and seasonings to taste in a large saucepan. 15 minutes over medium heat, until the cauliflower and quinoa are tender and fully cooked.
3. Remove from heat and blend in small batches using a blender. Be cautious; it will be extremely hot. 45 to 60 seconds are required for the blending procedure.

Asparagus Soup

Yield: 6 cups

Prep time: 10 minutes

Cook time: 20 minutes

> ½ teaspoon dried basil or 10 fresh basil leaves, chopped
>
> 4 cups chicken broth or stock
>
> 2 cups dehydrated asparagus
>
> 1 cup water
>
> 2 tablespoons butter or extra virgin olive oil
>
> salt and pepper, to taste

1. Place the asparagus and water in a saucepan and simmer over medium heat for five to ten minutes, or until the asparagus is tender. Drain and save the liquid from asparagus.
2. About one minute after adding the asparagus, butter, and basil to a stockpot over medium heat, the butter will melt.
3. Add the chicken stock and asparagus water to the stockpot and bring the mixture to a boil over high heat. Reduce heat to low and simmer for ten minutes. Remove from heat and allow to cool for five minutes.
4. Warm soup is poured into a blender in small batches and pureed to the desired consistency. After pureeing, transfer small portions to a large bowl so that they remain distinct. So that the soup has texture, I like to leave a few blender batches with larger chunks.
5. Return mixture to the stockpot and season to taste with salt and pepper.

Thermos Vegetable Soup

Yield: 2 cups

Prep time: 5 minutes

Cook time: 4 hours

> pinch onion powder
>
> salt and pepper, to taste
>
> 1 tablespoon spaghetti, broken into small sections
>
> ⅓ cup dried vegetables
>
> ¼ teaspoon dried parsley

¼ teaspoon dried sweet basil

pinch garlic powder

2 cups boiling chicken or beef broth

1. Boil water and fill an empty Thermos with it. Pour the hot water out just prior to placing the ingredients in the Thermos.
2. In a Thermos, combine the dried vegetables, parsley, basil, garlic powder, onion powder, salt, pepper, and pasta.
3. Pour the chicken or beef broth that has been brought to a boil over the dry ingredients. Cover the Thermos quickly and securely. Shake or flip the Thermos every hour until mealtime, if possible.

Sweet Potato Coconut Flour Pancakes

Yield: 6 medium pancakes

Prep time: 5 minutes

Cook time: 2 to 4 minutes

1 tablespoon granulated sugar or honey

¼ teaspoon baking powder

ground cinnamon, to taste

5 eggs

¼ cup milk

½ teaspoon vanilla extract

½ cup unsweetened applesauce

¼ cup coconut flour

¼ cup sweet potato flour

¼ teaspoon salt

1. Preheat a griddle or large skillet over medium heat.
2. Whisk together eggs, milk, vanilla, and applesauce in a large bowl.
3. In a medium bowl, thoroughly combine the coconut flour, sweet potato flour, sugar or honey, baking powder, cinnamon, and salt.
4. Add dry ingredients to wet ingredients. With a fork, combine the ingredients until there are no remaining lumps.
5. Ladle approximately 1/4 cup of batter at a time onto the hot griddle. Cook for two to four minutes per side until small bubbles appear on the surface, then flip.
6. Serve warm with toppings of your choosing.

Slow Cooker Stuffed Cabbage Rolls

Yield: 8 to 12 rolls

Prep time: 20 minutes

Cook time: 8 to 10 hours

1 tablespoon brown sugar (optional)

1 teaspoon Worcestershire sauce (optional)

1 cup cooked white rice

1 egg, beaten

8 to 12 dehydrated cabbage leaves

¼ cup dehydrated diced onion

⅔ cup tomato powder

1 pound extra-lean ground beef

1 teaspoon salt, plus more to taste

1 teaspoon pepper, plus more to taste

1. Bring water in a large pot to a boil. Add cabbage leaves that have been dehydrated and boil for 2 to 3 minutes, until soft. Drain and reserve.
2. In a small bowl, cover diced onion with hot water for approximately 15 minutes to rehydrate.
3. Put tomato powder in a medium bowl to prepare tomato sauce. Slowly pour in 2 cups of boiling water while whisking vigorously to break up any lumps. If desired, whisk in brown sugar and Worcestershire sauce. Set aside.
4. Combine cooked rice, egg, ground beef, onion, 2 tablespoons of tomato sauce, salt, and pepper in a large bowl. Stir with a spoon, or use clean hands to mash the mixture.
5. Place approximately a quarter cup of the mixture in each cabbage leaf, roll, and tuck the ends. Put rolls into the slow cooker.
6. Pour the remainder of the tomato sauce over the cabbage rolls. Cook covered on low for 8 to 10 hours.

Sautéed Winter Squash with Apples

Yield: 2 cups

Prep time: 1 hour

Cook time: 10 minutes

½ teaspoon celery salt

½ teaspoon garlic powder

½ teaspoon thyme

salt, to taste

1 cup dehydrated winter squash cubes

½ cup dehydrated onion

½ cup dehydrated apple

2 tablespoons butter

pepper, to taste

1. Cover the squash and onion cubes with 2 cups of warm water in a large bowl. Soak for 60 minutes. Remove any remaining liquid.
2. The apple can be rehydrated by placing it in a separate bowl and covering it with cool water for one hour.
3. In a large saucepan over medium heat, melt the butter.
4. Add the squash, onion, and celery salt to a saucepan and cook, stirring occasionally, for approximately 5 minutes, or until the squash begins to brown.
5. Add the apple and garlic powder and cook until the apple is tender, approximately 2 minutes.
6. To taste, add thyme, salt, and pepper.

Dehydrated Winter Squash Nests

Yield: 10 to 15 squash nests

Prep time: 30 minutes

Cook time: 4 to 6 hours

1 large winter squash, peeled and deseeded

1. Cut the squash into manageable pieces and shred it into long strands using a spiralizer. If you do not have a spiralizer, you can use a vegetable peeler to create thin, broad, noodle-like slices or a julienne peeler to create spaghetti-like strands.
2. Separate the pieces that form a continuous spiral by removing them from the stack.
3. Add the long strands to the dehydrator trays and form a nest by stacking each piece on top of the next. Add the smaller pieces to the dehydrator trays in small handfuls, 5 or 6 piles per tray, to form nests.
4. Dry at 140°F for two hours, then reduce heat to 130°F and continue drying for an additional two to four hours, or until pieces are brittle.

Garlic Creole Spiced Squash Nests

Yield: 10 nests

Prep time: 35 minutes

Cook time: 5 minutes

2 tablespoons olive oil

10 Dehydrated Winter Squash Nests, or 2 cups dried squash shreds

⅓ cup all-purpose flour

2 cloves garlic, minced

2 large eggs, beaten

1 tablespoon Creole Spice Blend

10 teaspoons cheddar cheese

1. Soak the squash nests in hot water for 30 minutes to rehydrate them. Remove and dispose of the soaking liquid.
2. Combine flour, garlic, eggs, and Creole seasoning in a large bowl. Carefully dunk the butternut squash nests in the egg mixture without breaking them apart.
3. In a large skillet over medium heat, heat the olive oil.
4. Remove one nest for each serving. In a skillet, place the squash and flatten it with a spatula. Cook until the underside is golden brown, about 2 minutes.
5. Flip and cook the other side for an additional 2 minutes.
6. Add 1 teaspoon of cheddar cheese to each nest and serve immediately.

CREOLE SPICE BLEND

Yield: about ½ cup

½ tablespoon black pepper

½ tablespoon white pepper

½ tablespoon cayenne pepper

2½ tablespoons paprika

1 tablespoon onion powder

1 tablespoon garlic powder

1 tablespoon dried basil

½ tablespoon dried thyme

1½ tablespoons salt

In a small bowl, combine onion powder, garlic powder, dried basil, dried thyme, pepper, paprika, and salt. Blend thoroughly

Fajita Beans and Rice

This blend is spicy; omit the cayenne pepper for a milder version.

Yield: 1 pint jar dry; 6 cups cooked

Prep time: 35 minutes

Cook time: 20 to 25 minutes

- *1 teaspoon chili powder*
- *½ teaspoon salt*
- *½ teaspoon paprika*
- *½ teaspoon brown sugar*
- *¼ teaspoon black pepper*
- *¼ teaspoon oregano*
- *¼ teaspoon cumin*
- *1 cup Quick Brown Rice*
- *2 cups Quick Cook Beans*
- *¼ cup dehydrated sweet bell pepper*
- *¼ cup dehydrated onion*
- *¼ cup dehydrated carrot*
- *¼ cup tomato powder*
- *¼ teaspoon dried garlic*
- *⅛ teaspoon cayenne pepper*

1. Place all of the ingredients in a 1-cup jar with a wide mouth or a Mylar bag. Add a 100cc oxygen absorber and tightly seal the container. Keep for up to five years.
2. Remove the oxygen packet and pour the contents of the jar into a large skillet before serving. Cover the vegetables with 6 cups of water and bring to a boil over high heat. Reduce heat to medium, cover, and simmer beans for 15 to 20 minutes, stirring occasionally, until tender.
3. To taste, garnish with grated cheese.

Riced Cauliflower Pizza Crust

This cauliflower crust is a nutritious alternative to standard pizza crusts. To reduce calories, replace a quarter of the cheese with a low-fat alternative.

Yield: 2 (8-inch) crusts

Prep time: 40 minutes

Cook time: 15 to 20 minutes

2 eggs

1 cup dehydrated cauliflower

4 cups water

2 cups grated Parmesan cheese

1. Preheat oven to 400 degrees Fahrenheit.
2. Place cauliflower in a large bowl, cover with four cups of hot water, and allow to soak for twenty minutes. Remove and dispose of the soaking liquid.
3. By hand or with a food processor, chop the rehydrated cauliflower until the pieces are small and uniform in size.
4. The cauliflower rice should be cooked in a skillet over medium heat. Stir until cauliflower is dry and moisture has been extracted.
5. Allow the cauliflower to cool before setting it aside. It may cool more quickly if removed from the pan.
6. Whisk the eggs in a different bowl. Incorporate Parmesan cheese.
7. Add cauliflower that has been cooled to the bowl, and stir until thoroughly combined.
8. On parchment paper, divide the mixture into two portions of equal size. Work each piece into an 8-inch diameter circle that is approximately 14 inch thick. Keep more of the mixture on the edges to ensure that the rounds cook evenly and do not burn on the edges.
9. Slide the parchment paper onto a baking sheet and bake at 400°F for 15 to 20 minutes, or until the rounds are browned and firm.

Ideas for Serving Cauliflower Crust

- *Spread with tomato sauce, herbs, cheese, and toppings for pizza. Bake for 10 to 15 minutes, or until the cheese melts and the toppings are heated through.*
- *With tomato sauce, herbs, and condiments. Roll into a log and bake for 15 minutes on parchment paper. Cheese, green onions, and sour cream are added on top. To serve, cut into 1-inch sections.*
- *Once the crust has cooled, cut it into sixteen equal strips. Sprinkle with your preferred spices (see Cajun Seasoning Blend on page 107) and reheat at 400 degrees Fahrenheit for ten minutes. The strips will be a delicious, crunchy snack.*

Hash Brown Mix in a Jar

Separately dry the ingredients and then combine them. This recipe makes one jar containing two meals.

Yield: 1 pint jar dry; 2 cups cooked

Prep time: 10 to 15 minutes

Cook time: 10 to 15 minutes

¼ cup dried minced garlic

2 cups dehydrated potato shreds

½ cup dried onion

½ cup dried sweet pepper

1 teaspoon vegetable oil

1. In a large bowl, combine the potato shreds, dried onion, dried sweet pepper, and dried minced garlic. Place the ingredients in a canning jar or Mylar bag. Add a 100cc oxygen absorber and tightly seal the container. Keep for up to five years.
2. Pour 1 cup of the contents of the jar into a bowl, cover with boiling water, and let stand for 10 to 15 minutes until plump. Squeeze and press to remove excess water.
3. Heat oil in a skillet over medium heat.
4. While cooking, press the potato mixture into a thin, even layer in the skillet.
5. Approximately 3 minutes per side are required to achieve a crisp exterior.

Quick Brown Rice

Store dehydrated rice in canning jars containing 100cc oxygen absorbers, or remove oxygen using the FoodSaver accessory. Due to brown rice's high fat content, Quick Brown Rice should be consumed within six months.

Yield: 2 cups dehydrated rice; 3½ cups cooked rice

Prep time: 5 to 7 hours

Cook time: 17 minutes

1. Cook 2 cups of regular brown rice according to the instructions on the package; absorb all liquid.
2. Spread the cooked rice in a single layer on dehydrator trays lined with parchment paper or Paraflexx liners. Dehydrate for 5 to 7 hours at 125°F. In the middle of the drying process, separate any rice that has adhered together and rotate the trays. When the rice is completely dry, it should click when dropped onto a tabletop.
3. To rehydrate, place one cup of dried rice in a saucepan and cover with three-quarters cup of water. Soak for five minutes to start the rehydration process, then bring to a boil and boil for two minutes. Remove from heat, cover, and allow to rest for ten minutes. Fluff the rice with a fork.

Quick Cook Beans

Yield: 3 cups

Prep time: 10 minutes, plus 8 hours

Cook time: 8 to 10 hours

4 cups dry beans

1. Soak dried beans overnight. Discard water.
2. After soaking the beans for at least eight hours, place them in a large pot, cover with water, and bring to a boil. Reduce heat to low and simmer for ten minutes. Drain.
3. Spread the partially cooked beans in a single layer on dehydrator trays and process at 95 to 100 degrees Fahrenheit for eight to ten hours. They will be rigid after drying
4. Store in canning jars with 100cc oxygen absorbers or remove oxygen using the FoodSaver accessory. The product has a shelf life of five years.

Mrs. B's Stovetop Baked Beans

Yield: 3 cups

Prep time: 15 minutes

Cook time: 10 minutes

¼ cup dehydrated chopped onion

2 teaspoons mustard

1 cup Quick Cook Beans

2 cups water

⅛ cup packed brown sugar, or to taste

1 teaspoon Worcestershire sauce

1. Rehydrate the Quick Cook Beans by soaking them in 2 cups of water for 5 minutes in a saucepan. Bring the liquid to a boil for 10 minutes. Avoid covering.
2. Add the remaining ingredients to the dish. Stir the brown sugar until it has dissolved.
3. Reduce the heat to medium and continue to simmer for an additional 5 minutes, or until the beans are tender and the sauce has formed. If necessary, add additional water in increments of 1 teaspoon.

Mexican Fiesta Bake

Yield: 1 (2½-quart) baking dish

Prep time: 45 minutes

Cook time: 15 minutes

2 fresh jalapeño peppers

2 cups ground beef

1 teaspoon garlic

1 lime, juiced

6 corn tortillas, cut into 1-inch squares

1 cup dehydrated tomatoes

1 cup fresh or dehydrated cilantro leaves

½ cup dehydrated, diced green pepper

½ cup dehydrated corn kernels

¼ cup tomato powder

1 cup cheddar cheese

1. Preheat oven to 350 degrees Fahrenheit.
2. Cover the dehydrated tomatoes with 2 cups of cool water in a small bowl for 30 minutes, or until plump and tender. Drain and dice into bite-sized pieces.
3. Add enough cool water to cover the cilantro leaves, diced green pepper, and corn in a small bowl. Allow peppers to soak for 10 to 15 minutes, or until plump. Drain.
4. To make tomato sauce, slowly combine 14 cup tomato powder with 12 ounces of hot water. Blend until uniform. Set aside.
5. Remove the seeds from 2 fresh jalapeo peppers and dice them.
6. In a large skillet, cook the ground beef until it is completely browned.
7. To the ground beef, add the tomato sauce, garlic, lime juice, tomato, cilantro, green pepper, corn, tortillas, and jalapeno. Mix and heat thoroughly.
8. Transfer to a baking dish measuring 212 quarts and top with cheese.
9. Bake the cheese for 15 minutes, or until bubbly.

Rose Hip Mint Tea

Rose hips contain more vitamin C than citrus fruits on average. They are sweet and could be used to make tea on their own, but adding mint makes this beverage even more refreshing. This recipe is also an excellent remedy for stomach ailments and bloating.

Do not discard the rose hips after using them to make tea. Consume them instead. Rose hips retain their nutritional value, so after you have finished drinking the tea, add them to soups or serve them as a side dish.

Yield: 1 cup

Prep time: 0 minutes

Steep time: 10 to 15 minutes

  1 teaspoon dried rose hips

  1 teaspoon dried spearmint or peppermint

  1 cup water

1. In a French press or teapot, combine the mint and rose hips with 1 cup of hot water. Some teamakers grind their rose hips prior to using them, but it is not required.
2. Infuse for 10 to 15 minutes while covered. The longer the steeping time, the deeper the flavor and color.

Orange Mint Tea Blend

Yield: 1 cup

Prep time: 5 minutes, plus rest time

Steep time: 10 minutes

  2 tablespoons dried orange

  2 tablespoons dried, chopped mint

  3 or 4 whole cloves (optional)

1. In a coffee grinder or mortar and pestle, pulverize the dry ingredients until the pieces are uniform in size. Allow the flavor to develop over several days in a jar with a tight-fitting lid.
2. Add 1 milliliter of Orange Mint Tea. Pour the mixture into a tea ball infuser, teapot, or French press. Cover and infuse for ten minutes. This makes a refreshing iced tea as well.

Lemon Verbena Sun Tea

Lemon verbena is known as a digestive herb in traditional medicine. It assists in alleviating indigestion, flatulence, and colic. It is mildly astringent, and using it to make a mouth rinse can help prevent candidiasis.

Yield: 1 quart

Prep time: 0 minutes

Steep time: several hours

  1 handful dried lemon verbena leaves

  1 quart water

1. Add a handful of crushed dried leaves to a large glass jar.
2. Cover the leaves with 1 quart of water and leave the jar in direct sunlight for several hours.
3. To make a refreshing drink, strain the leaves and combine them with ice.

Lemonade with Dehydrated Citrus

Yield: 5 quarts

Prep time: 0 minutes

Cook time: 3 hours rest time

5 quarts water

1 cup sugar

15 pieces dehydrated citrus rounds

1. Stir sugar into 5 quarts of water until dissolved.
2. Add citrus pieces and mix thoroughly.
3. Add ice to maintain the submersion of the rinds. Allow it to rest at least 3 hours.
4. Stir, then strain into glasses garnished with rehydrated citrus rounds.

Apple Crisp with Oat Topping

Yield: 1 (8 × 8-inch) glass pan

Prep time: 35 minutes

Cook time: 30 minutes

½ cup flour

½ cup oats

pinch salt

⅛ teaspoon ground cinnamon, plus more, to taste

3 cups dehydrated apple slices

¾ cup sugar, divided

2 tablespoons cornstarch

½ stick cold butter

1. Preheat oven to 375 degrees Fahrenheit. Spray a glass pan measuring 8 by 8 inches with cooking spray.
2. Place the apple slices in a bowl and cover with boiling water. Let it sit for 30 minutes.

Reserve the liquid that has been drained.

3. Mix 12 cup sugar and cinnamon to taste with the rehydrated apples.
4. In a measuring cup, thoroughly combine cornstarch and 2 tablespoons of cold water until no lumps remain.
5. Cook the apples and reserved liquid for five minutes in a medium saucepan. Add the cornstarch slurry and heat the mixture until it becomes thick. If the apples appear too dry, add additional liquid, 1 tablespoon at a time, until you achieve the desired consistency.
6. Spoon the apples into the prepared pan and press them down to ensure that they are coated with the sauce.
7. Add the flour, oats, remaining sugar, salt, and 1/8 teaspoon of cinnamon to a small bowl to make the topping. Using a pastry blender or food processor, combine the butter and dry ingredients until the mixture resembles coarse crumbs.
8. Pour the topping over the apple filling and evenly distribute to the edges. Bake until the topping is golden brown and the filling is bubbling for 30 minutes.

Steve's Low-Fat Pineapple Cake

This family-favorite recipe has been modified for low-fat diets. It is not excessively sweet, but it satisfies your sweet tooth.

Yield: 1 (8 × 8-inch) cake

Prep time: 25 minutes

Cook time: 25 to 30 minutes

2 teaspoons vanilla extract

2 eggs

1 (3.5-ounce) package sugar-free vanilla instant pudding

4 cups dehydrated pineapple

2 cups water

2¼ cups all-purpose flour

1 cup granulated sugar

2 teaspoons baking soda

pinch salt

1½ cups fat-free whipped cream

1. Preheat oven to 350 degrees Fahrenheit. Coat with butter and flour an 8 x 8-inch baking dish.
2. Crush the dehydrated pineapple with a rolling pin or a food processor in a plastic bag with a zip-top closure. The pineapple should be in chunks, not as a powder. Save two

cups.

3. Cover the remaining crushed pineapple with 2 cups of cool tap water in a small bowl for 15 to 20 minutes. Add additional water if necessary. Drain and reserve the liquid from the pineapple.
4. Whisk together the flour, sugar, baking soda, and salt in a medium bowl.
5. Combine the vanilla extract and eggs with the rehydrated pineapple in a small bowl.
6. Stir together the wet and dry ingredients until a batter forms.
7. Pour the batter into the dish that has been prepared.
8. Bake for 25 to 30 minutes, or until a toothpick inserted into the cake comes out golden brown. Allow to cool prior to adding topping.
9. Whisk together the 2 cups of crushed pineapple, pineapple liquid, and sugar-free pudding mix. Add additional water in increments of 1 teaspoon, if necessary. Fold the whipping cream in gently until incorporated.
10. Spread frosting on top of the cake. Refrigerate until serving time.

Candied Ginger

The ginger syrup from step 5 can be stored in the refrigerator for up to two months. If the syrup runs out, you can use the candied ginger to make more.

Yield: 8 ounces candied ginger

Prep time: 40 minutes, plus 1 hour conditioning time

Cook time: 4 to 6 hours

1 large (8-ounce) ginger root

4 cups water

2¼ cups sugar, divided

1. Peel and wash the ginger root. Mandoline the root into 1/8-inch-thick slices.
2. Stir 4 cups water and 2 cups sugar until the sugar is dissolved in the saucepan.
3. Bring the ginger to a boil in the saucepan before adding the pieces.
4. Reduce the heat to a simmer and cook for 30 minutes, allowing steam to escape by leaving the saucepan partially uncovered.
5. The ginger mixture is strained, and the syrup is saved in a canning jar.
6. Place the ginger pieces on a rack or dehydrator tray for one hour, or until they are sticky but not wet, to condition.
7. Toss the pieces until they are lightly coated with the remaining 14 cup sugar. You can omit this step and reduce the amount of sugar; they will still taste sweet due to the simple syrup.
8. Place ginger slices on the dehydrator tray and dry at 135 degrees Fahrenheit for four to

six hours, or until the pieces are pliable but not internally sticky.

Oatmeal Fig Cookies

Fig and oatmeal are a natural pairing. Add fruit to your favorite recipe or use this timeless classic.

Yield: 2 dozen cookies

Prep time: 10 minutes, plus 1 hour chill time

Cook time: 12 to 14 minutes

- 1 cup butter, softened to room temperature
- 1 cup packed brown sugar
- ½ cup granulated sugar
- 2 eggs
- 1 teaspoon vanilla extract
- 1 ½ cups all-purpose flour
- 1 teaspoon baking powder
- ½ teaspoon salt
- 3 cups old-fashioned rolled oats (for a softer cookie, process half the oats in a blender until finely ground)
- 1 cup rehydrated figs, cut into pieces

1. Preheat oven to 350 degrees Fahrenheit. Baking sheets are lined with parchment paper.
2. Whisk together the flour, baking powder, and salt in a large bowl. Stir the oats in.
3. Using a hand mixer, cream the butter and sugars in another large bowl. Add the eggs and vanilla, then cream the mixture once more.
4. Add the flour mixture to the liquid, then combine with a stir. Incorporate the rehydrated fig chunks.
5. Refrigerate the dough for one hour or overnight.
6. Place tablespoon-sized scoops on the baking sheets, leaving 2 inches between each cookie. 12 to 14 minutes, or until cookies are lightly golden brown.

ABOUT THE AUTHOR

Melinda Baker is a qualified expert in the preservation of food. She educates others on how to properly cook and store nutritious meals, how to live a simple life while maintaining their integrity, and how to make the most of what they already have. Her day job is in publishing, and she makes her home in a rural area of Utah. Cooking, spinning, and knitting are among Linda's favorite hobbies, and she adores spending time with her children and grandchildren.

Printed in Great Britain
by Amazon